The Write Ingredients

Recipes From Your Favorite Authors

Lori Foster

A Samhain Publishing, Ltd. publication.

Samhain Publishing, Ltd.
512 Forest Lake Drive
Warner Robins, GA 31093
www.samhainpublishing.com

The Write Ingredients: Recipes From Your Favorite Authors
Copyright © 2007 by Lori Foster
Print ISBN: 1-59998-653-1
Digital ISBN: 1-59998-652-3

Cover by Dawn Seewer

First Samhain Publishing, Ltd. electronic publication: June 2007
First Samhain Publishing, Ltd. print publication: June 2007

Hello readers!

   As an annual "thank you" to readers and authors alike, Dianne Castell and I have organized a June "Reader & Author" event in Ohio. We have a great turnout with lots of authors, editors, agents, and readers. We do a fabulous raffle with proceeds going to worthy organizations. http://lorifoster.com/community/readergettogthr.htm. *It's a fun, casual time for everyone to visit, share a love of books, and help others.*

   *In addition to that, my reader group, Lori Foster Bookjunkys—*LoriFosterBookjunkys-subscribe@yahoogroups.com—*has been hard at work doing a "troop project." Through generous donations and the organizational finesse of our fabulous volunteer, Laurie Damron, we buy and ship fun, heartwarming, and sometimes necessary items to our beloved troops.*

   This cookbook is our way of furthering our contribution. Over 90 authors, and a handful of dedicated readers, have offered up their favorite recipes for you. All initial proceeds will go toward the "troop project," and should the proceeds exceed our expectations, other charitable organizations will be chosen.

   Thank you for doing your part to help us honor our brave soldiers, and others in need.

   My best,

Lori Foster

Contents

Appetizers & Beverages

Jenny Gardiner
www.jennygardiner.net

Sun-dried Tomato Dip

Ingredients:

12 sun-dried tomatoes (packed in oil)
7-oz. (1 jar) roasted red peppers, drained
1 clove garlic, minced
1 tbsp. chopped parsley
1 tbsp. lemon juice
1/2 tsp. ground pepper
dash salt
4 oz. cream cheese, softened and cubed
1/2 cup sour cream

Directions:

Rinse & pat dry tomatoes and red peppers. In food processor with blade, chop garlic and parsley. Add tomatoes and peppers then puree. Add lemon juice, salt and pepper. Add cream cheese and sour cream. Process till smooth, scraping sides of bowl to mix thoroughly. Serve immediately, or cover and chill. Serve on baguette slices.

Toni Blake
www.toniblake.com

Toni Blake's Fabulous Chicken Spread

Ingredients

10 oz. canned chicken
8 oz. chive & onion cream cheese
4 tbsp. mayonnaise
2 tbsp. minced onion spice
1 1/2 tsp. soy sauce
1/2 tsp. salt

Directions:

Let cream cheese soften 1 hour. Drain chicken. Combine all ingredients using a fork. Chill. Place in bowl next to a plate of your favorite crackers along with a knife or spreader. Enjoy!

Susan Kearney
www.susankearney.com

Susan Kearney's Favorite Barbeque Sauce

Ingredients & Directions:

Mix one packet onion Lipton soup, one bottle of Red Russian Dressing, one jar apricot preserves.

Spoon over barbeque ribs or chicken.

Ann M. Warner

www.annwarner.com

Black Bean Dip

This colorful and healthy dip is always a hit. I've never served it without someone asking for the recipe which I got from a friend who lives in Puerto Rico and has a mango tree in her backyard.

Ingredients & Directions

Toss together:
1 can drained, rinsed black beans
1 1/2 cup of diced ripe or frozen mangoes (fresh or frozen peaches may be substituted)
2 tbsp. grated ginger (1/4 tsp. of ginger spice may be substituted)
2 tbsp. fresh cilantro, chopped
1/4 cup diced red onion
1 Jalapeno pepper, seeded and diced
Juice of 1 lime or 1 lemon

Serve with tortilla chips.

Kay Stockham
www.kaystockham.com

Lebanese Marinade

Ingredients:

3/4 cup olive oil
1/2 cup lemon juice
4 cloves garlic
1 tsp. salt
1 tsp. paprika
pepper to taste
(will season 2 lbs. of chicken)

Great to serve with salad.

Catherine Mann
www.CatherineMann.com

Cream Cheese & Ham Ball

Ingredients:

1 – 8 oz. pkg. cream cheese
1 – 6 3/4 oz. can Hormel chunk ham
1/4 cup mayo or Miracle Whip
1/4 tsp. dry mustard
2 tbsp. Parsley Flakes
1 tbsp. minced onions or 2 stalks green onions chopped

Directions:

Mix together and roll in chopped pecans. Serve with crackers.

Mary Campisi
www.marycampisi.com

Buffalo Chicken Dip

Ingredients:

1 cup of ranch dressing—blue cheese works, too.
1 cup of Frank's hot wing sauce
2 - 8 oz. pkg. cream cheese
2 cans of chunk chicken (the bigger size, I think they are 12.5 oz. I get at Costco), drained and chopped

Directions:

Mix in large bowl
Bake at 350 degrees for 20 minutes
(Option- some people put shredded cheddar cheese on top and bake, I choose not too) Serve with tortilla chips, celery, thin sliced baguettes or whatever.
Note: If you want really 'hot' dip, use Frank's hot sauce instead of Frank's hot wing sauce.

Lisa Freeman - Reader
"This dip is as spicy as one of Erin McCarthy's vamps!"

Hot Cheese Dip

Ingredients:

1 large block Velveeta
1 pound Italian sausage, cooked, drained, crumbled
2 cans Ro-Tel tomatoes

Put everything in the crock pot for several hours. If in a hurry, melt cheese on low heat stirring often, then add sausage and tomatoes. Once combined, remove from heat.

Serve with Tostitos or Fritos.

Cindy Cruciger
www.CindyCruciger.com

Meatballs & Sauce

Ingredients:

Meatballs:

3 pounds ground pork
2 – 8 oz. cans drained, finely chopped water chestnuts
1 1/2 cups finely chopped green onions
1 tbsp. finely chopped fresh or crystallized ginger
2 tbsp. salt
3 tbsp. soy sauce
4 lightly beaten eggs
1 1/2 cups bread crumbs
1/4 cup cornstarch
1/2 cups vegetable oil

Sauce:

1 – 8 oz. can chopped pineapple
2 cups unsweetened pineapple juice
1 cup cider vinegar
1/4 cup soy sauce
2/3 cup sugar
1 1/2 cups beef broth
2 tbsp. finely chopped fresh or crystallized ginger
1/3 cup cornstarch
2/3 cup cold water

Directions:

Combine pork, water chestnuts, green onion, 1 tbsp. ginger, salt, 3 tablespoons soy sauce and eggs in a large bowl. Mix well with hands.

Add bread crumbs and mix until just combined, chill mixture.

Shape into 3/4 to 1 inch balls, roll the balls in cornstarch.

Brown meat on all sides in hot oil. Remove balls and put on a roasting pan.

To freeze, place meatballs in a single layer on the roasting pan and put into freezer bags when frozen. Take out a needed.

Preheat oven to 350 degrees and bake meatballs for 15 to 20 minutes until cooked through.

To make sauce, combine pineapple with juice, vinegar, 1/4 cup soy sauce, 2/3 cup sugar, beef broth and ginger in large saucepan, bring to boiling.

Mix cornstarch with cold water, add to boiling mixture stirring constantly. Continue cooking and stirring until sauce is thick and clear.

Sauce will keep in refrigerator for up to a week.

To serve, place in chafing dish with enough sauce to coat balls. Serve with toothpicks!

Note: Make sure you set these on a table by themselves with 360 degree access because the party guests ball up around them until they are gone.

Marcia James
www.MarciaJames.net

Avocado Body Paint

Ingredients:

4 ripe avocados – halved & pitted
6 tbsp. of sour cream
1 tsp. of salt
Sprinkling of cayenne pepper
2 tsp. of lemon juice

Directions:

Put the flesh of the avocado in a food processor and pulse to roughly chop up the avocado. Add the sour cream. Pulse until the mixture is the texture of yogurt. Add the salt, cayenne pepper and lemon juice. Pulse until smooth. The recipe makes approximately 2 cups of avocado body paint – or a couple cups of avocado dip, if you choose to serve it with chips!

Author Note:

Avocados have long been considered an aphrodisiac and are, therefore, an ideal ingredient for edible body paint. The Aztecs believed avocados, hanging in pairs on the trees, resembled a man's "family jewels." Be forewarned, however, that using this chilled mixture on the aforementioned organ could result in unwanted shrinkage. Also, covering the bed with a plastic shower curtain liner is recommended before application!

Anne Rainey
http://annerainey.com

Jarlsberg Cheese Dip

Ingredients:

1 cup sweet onion, peeled and chopped
2 cups mayonnaise
2 cups Jarlsberg cheese

Directions:

You'll want to buy a block of cheese and shred it at home for the best flavor. Then, in a large mixing bowl, combine the mayonnaise and cheese, while slowly adding in the onion. I've found it's best to add a 1/4 cup of onion at a time, until you get the desired tang you're looking for. Some like a lot of onion, while others like just a hint.

Author Note:

The dip is best served after the flavors have had time to blend, so chill in the refrigerator for a couple of hours. Serve with a good bottle of Chianti and sesame seed crackers. It's a feast for your palette, let me tell you!

Lori Foster
www.lorifoster.com

Vegetable Pizza

Ingredients:

1 pkg. crescent rolls
1 pkg. cream cheese
1 pkg. Hidden Valley Ranch dry dressing mix
Assortment of veggies, diced small, your preference

Directions:

Preheat oven according to crescent roll package.
Unroll crescent rolls and flatten into a round pizza pan, making sure edges are secured and that the dough goes all the way to the outer edge of the pan.
Bake according to package directions.
Note: Do not over bake!
Remove and let cool.
Mix cream cheese and Hidden Valley Ranch dry dressing mix.
Spread evenly over cool crescent roll "pizza" crust.
Place vegetables on top.
I like to use:
Slivered carrots
Chopped cauliflower
Chopped broccoli
Bean sprouts

Cut into thin slices. Makes a great appetizer!

Author Note:

I choose those vegetables because they're readily available at all grocery salad bars, and make a nice mixture of colors and textures for the pizza. But you can also add mushrooms, onions, whatever is your favorite!

Gemma Bruce
www.gemmabruce.com

Southern Cheese Sausage Biscuits

Ingredients:

2 1/4 cups Bisquick
1/2 cup milk
1 cup shredded sharp cheese
1 cup crumbled bulk sausage

Directions:

Brown sausage, crumbling it into fine pieces, when fully cooked set on a paper towel to drain.
Mix Bisquick, milk and cheese.
When thoroughly mixed, add cooled sausage.

You can adjust the amount of Bisquick depending on whether you want drop or rolled biscuits. Dropped biscuit dough is sticky to the touch. Drop a heaping tbsp. amount onto an ungreased cookie sheet, leaving room for biscuits to expand.

For rolled biscuits, add enough Bisquick to make the mixture easy to handle. Place on a floured board and knead 10-15 times (over kneading will make biscuits tough). Roll to desired height, cut with a floured biscuit cutter or jelly jar and place on an ungreased cookie sheet two inches apart.

Bake at 375 degrees from 10 to 15 minutes or until golden brown.

Great with soups or can be shaped smaller for the party tray.

Author Note:

My grandmother use to make these from scratch. I've substituted Bisquick for a faster prep time.

Lisa Freeman - Reader
This casserole is as unique as a Christine Feehan
Carpathian hero.

Pineapple Cheese Casserole

Ingredients:

1 can pineapple tidbits, drained, reserve juice
3 tbsp. flour
3 tbsp. pineapple juice
3 tbsp. sugar
1 cup shredded sharp cheddar cheese
1/3 cup melted butter
1/2 cup buttery cracker crumbs (Ritz, Townhouse, etc.)

Directions:

Preheat oven to 350 degrees. Drain pineapple, reserving 3 tablespoons juice. Combine sugar and flour; stir in juice. Add cheese and pineapple tidbits. Mix well. Spoon into greased 1 quart casserole. Combine melted butter with cracker crumbs. Sprinkle over pineapple mixture. Bake 20-30 minutes. Serves 4. Can easily be doubled or tripled.

Stacy Ahlgren - Reader

A yummy snack to eat while reading a new
Stella Cameron novel.

Taco Dip

Ingredients:

1 can of Hormel chili, no beans (turkey chili can be substituted)
1 pkg. of softened Philly cream cheese (can be fat-free or 1/3 fat)
1 pkg. (2-3 cups) of mild shredded cheddar cheese (can be different flavor and/or reduced fat)

Directions:

In a glass pie plate, layer with softened cream cheese, add the chili, and top with the cheese. Nuke it for 3 + minutes and serve with tortilla chips (El Ranchero no salt chips are awesome!) Better make 2! Enjoy.

Catherine Spaulding

Ann's quick snack or light lunch.

Ingredients & Directions:

Large Chips, any kind about 8
Top with 3 chopped green onions
Cover with canned hot chili beans
Top with shredded cheese, like cheddar.
Microwave one minute

Joanne Rock
www.joannerock.com

Strawberry Iced Tea Fizz

Ingredients:

1 pint basket fresh strawberries, stemmed and sliced
1/2 cup sugar
5 cups of boiling water
1 orange pekoe tea bag
1 can (12 ounces) frozen lemonade concentrate, thawed
1 qt. chilled sparkling water
Ice cubes

Directions:

In large bowl combine strawberries and sugar, set aside. In another bowl pour water over tea bag, steep 5 minutes. Discard tea bag; cool tea to room temperature. Stir tea into strawberry mixture along with lemonade concentrate; chill. To serve, stir in sparkling water, ladle over ice cubes in tall glasses. Serve with spoons.
Author Note: A tea party favorite!

Susanne Marie Knight
www.susanneknight.com

Finest Wine of Poseidia or Mulled Wine

Ingredients:

1 gal. Burgundy wine
1 orange, sliced & stuck with cloves
2 cinnamon sticks
1 lemon, sliced & stuck with cloves
6 allspice corns
1 cup sugar

Directions:

Combine all ingredients in large *enamel* pot or slow cooker.
Gently stir.
Heat on lowest heat possible for 4 to 5 hours.

Author Note: In my paranormal romantic suspense PAST INDISCRETIONS, Savannah's first visit to Atlantis includes a glass of the finest wine of Poseidia, made from the choicest of red grapes. As impossible as it sounds, when she returns from her "trip," back to the past, her lips are stained purple. Here is a delicious recipe for heated, spiced wine that will bring a smile to your own lips!

Susanne Marie Knight
www.susanneknight.com

Bloody Red Juice or Cranberry Punch

Ingredients:

2 pints cranberry juice cocktail, chilled
3 tbsp. sugar
2 cup pineapple juice, chilled
2 qts. ginger ale, chilled

Directions:

Combine juices in large punch bowl.
Stir in sugar.
Add ginger ale when ready to serve.

Author Note: In the best-selling romantic paranormal suspense GRAVE FUTURE, Dan advises Velma to drink cranberry juice, which is high in vitamin C and helpful to someone in her condition. The red stain from the juice eerily contrasts with the unnatural paleness of her skin. While this recipe might not give your lips a chilling red glow, it's a guaranteed thirst quencher on a hot, summer day.

Tori Carrington
www.toricarrington.net
www.sofiemetro.com

Traditional Greek Coffee

Ingredients:

1 full tsp. Greek coffee powder (found at any Greek shop)
1 tsp. sugar (to taste)
1 cup of water (measure using the cup you plan to serve
the coffee in, increasing the above ingredients the large
the cup)

Directions:

Add coffee and sugar to water in a briki (small coffee pan).
Stir over low heat until mixed. Let rise to the top. Serve. *Stin
eyeia sas!*

Author Note:

Food plays such a huge role in Greek and Greek-American
life. It's more than the source of fuel for the body, it's a salve for
the soul, an excuse to bring family and friends together. A brief
stop can easily turn into an hour long visit, usually resulting in
empty plates, laughter and happy memories.

Larissa Lyons
www.larissalyons.com

Tangy French Dressing
(original recipe from Larissa Lyons)

Ingredients & Directions:

Mix dry ingredients in small bowl:

1/4 tbsp. chopped, dried onion
1/2 tsp. dry mustard
1/2 tsp. paprika
1/2 tsp. garlic powder
1/2 tsp. celery seed (or powder)

Using a funnel and starting with the oil, measure the following into a 12 oz. glass bottle or jar:

2/3 cup safflower oil
1/4 cup honey
1/3 cup vinegar
1 1/2 tsp. molasses
2 tbsp. tomato sauce (or ketchup!)

Remove the funnel, add in the dry ingredients, and shake. Store in the fridge. I use this instead of store-bought dressings full of gunk I can't spell—or say! :)

Susan Elizabeth Phillips
www.susanephillips.com

REN GAGE'S Classic Marinara

Ingredients:

1 large onion, chopped
1 red pepper, chopped
1 pound of mushrooms, rough sliced
4 cloves of garlic, chopped
1 can (28 oz.) whole tomatoes (chopped or processed in food processor)
1 can (15 oz.) tomato sauce
1 tbsp. dried basil, dried oregano, sugar
1 tsp. dried thyme, rosemary
1/2 tsp. crushed red pepper
(options: Capers, spinach, eggplant in any combination. Meat can also be added according to preference.)

Directions:

Sauté vegetables, garlic, and spices in a little olive oil until soft. Add tomatoes and tomato sauce. Heat to a boil over medium heat, then reduce to low and cook about 1 hour. Serve over rotini or your favorite pasta. Garnish with parmesan or feta.

Author Note:

The hero of *Breathing Room*, Ren Gage, is Hollywood's favorite villain. He's also half Italian, and when he was a child, his nonna tried to keep him out of trouble by teaching him to cook. Here is a Classic Marinara recipe guaranteed to make your home smell like an Italian cucina. It has the added advantage of being low fat, vegetarian, easy to prepare, and multi purpose. A Phillips Family staple, I must have made this 1001 times. You may vary the vegetables you chose according to preference. Food processor speeds preparation.

Brenda Williamson
www.BrendaWilliamson.com

Smokey Salmon Dip

Ingredients:

8 oz. cream cheese, softened
7-8 oz. pink salmon, drained, flaked, and cartilage removed
3 tbsp. chopped fresh parsley
4 tbsp. finely chopped green bell pepper
2 tsp. grated onion
1 tsp. lemon juice
1 tsp. prepared horseradish
1/2 tsp. liquid smoke
Optional: 1/2 cup finely chopped pecans

Directions:

In a mixing bowl, combine all ingredients. Mix until well blended. Serve on favorite crackers.

Author Note:

This is great with any crackers that you can dip or as a spread on cocktail bread for larger appetizers. It's firmer when chilled for several hours.

Brenda Williamson
www.BrendaWilliamson.com

Stuffing Balls

Ingredients:

2 lbs. stuffing mix (like Stove Top), chicken flavor, fix as directed.
Cut up 2 loaves white sandwich bread into cubes.
4 chicken bouillon cubes dissolved in 2 cups of hot water
1/2 stick butter, melted
6 Bouillon cubes
1/2 stick butter, melted
flour water for thickening
Kitchen Bouquet (or any gravy browning liquid)

Directions:

Mix first 4 ingredients together. Shape loosely with hands into baseball size balls. Put balls into a shallow pan so they don't quite touch each other. Make gravy by cooking next 4 ingredients in sauce pan. Pour gravy over stuffing balls.

Bake in preheated oven 350 degrees for 1/2 hour.

Author Note:

This is a great side dish for large gatherings and goes well with roasted chicken or any other roasted meats.

Soups, Salads & Breads

Mia King
www.miaking.com

Orgasmic Corn Fritters with Chinese Peppercorn, Crème Fraîche and Sherry

William uses fresh Chinese peppercorn from China, but you can substitute red chili flakes or experiment with other local peppercorn varieties. This orgasmic response helped Deidre shape her future – imagine what it can do for you!

Serves 4.

Ingredients:

1 cup plus 2 tsp. all-purpose flour
1/4 tsp. baking powder
1 egg
1 cup fresh corn kernels, off the cob
2 tbsp. red bell pepper, finely chopped
1/8 tsp. Chinese peppercorn, crushed (or substitute dried red chili flakes)
1/4 cup crème fraîche
1/4 cup sherry
1 tbsp. extra virgin olive oil

Directions:

In a large bowl, mix flour, baking powder, egg, corn, bell pepper, sherry, Chinese peppercorn and crème fraîche. Bring a skillet to medium high heat; add olive oil. Drop spoonfuls of batter, forming four fritters, cooking until bottoms are lightly browned, about 3 minutes. Flip carefully and cook an additional 2 minutes. Drain any excess oil and serve.

Mia King
www.miaking.com

Uptown Bistro's Spinach Salad with Light Roquefort Dressing

The Uptown Bistro didn't get a lot of things right, but this one was a winner. Try it, and you'll see why Caroline cleaned her plate before sticking Deidre with the bill.

Serves 8.

Spinach Salad

Ingredients:

1 1/2 lbs. spinach, stems removed, washed
2 tbsp. sliced almonds
4 hard-boiled egg whites, coarsely chopped
8 mushrooms, sliced

Directions:

Toast slivered almonds for 3 to 5 minutes in a preheated 300 degree oven. Wash and pat dry spinach leaves, tearing into bite-size pieces. Toss with Light Roquefort Dressing (see below) and serve on individual plates. Top with almonds, egg whites, and sliced mushrooms.

Light Roquefort Dressing

Ingredients:

6 oz. Roquefort cheese (the better the cheese, the better the
   dressing)
1 cup thick, nonfat yogurt cheese (made from 3 cups
   nonfat yogurt –see below)
2 tbsp. low-fat mayonnaise
freshly ground pepper to taste

Directions:

Mix Roquefort, yogurt cheese, and mayonnaise together.
   Season with pepper.

Making Yogurt Cheese

Yogurt cheese is a healthy alternative to sour cream, cream
cheese, or mayonnaise. It requires some advance preparation
but can be stored for up to the life of the yogurt. To make 1 cup
of yogurt cheese, place 2 to 3 cups nonfat yogurt in a yogurt
strainer or cheesecloth. This will remove any excess water,
thickening the yogurt. Let drain 12-24 hours in the refrigerator,
checking occasionally until desired thickness is achieved.

Refrigerate any unused portion.

Queen Janeen aka Janeen Coyle of radio 103.5

Janeen's Special Day Turkey Wild Rice Soup
(made on Christmas Eve by Janeen's daughter-in-law Katie and then by Janeen!)

Ingredients:

4 cups chicken stock
2/3 cup diced carrots, mushrooms and onions
1 cup diced turkey (Hormel canned or turkey breast)
2-3 strips thick sliced bacon (diced)
3 tbsp. butter
1 1/2 cup heavy cream
1 tbsp. flour
1 pkg. of Uncle Ben's herb & wild rice boxed rice

Directions:

Sauté rice, carrots, onions, mushrooms and bacon in 2 tbsp butter for 5 minutes.

Add chicken stock, diced turkey, and all the contents of the Uncle Ben's rice box, including the seasoning packet.

Heat, stirring occasionally, for 45 minutes.

Stir in heavy cream with a wire whisk.

In a separate bowl, mash remaining butter and flour-until it is totally mixed. Using wire whisk, stir this into the soup until thickened and simmer for one minute.

Viola! Yummy with hot French bread or crackers. Serve as an appetizer or as a meal. Feel free to add or subtract any ingredients you want.

Sylvia Day
www.SylviaDay.com
www.DreamGuardians.com

Almost-a-Dessert-Cornbread

Ingredients:

1 large can of Mexicorn (undrained)
1 (16 oz.) can of creamed corn
1 box Jiffy Corn Muffin Mix
1 cup sour cream
1 stick of melted butter (best to use actual butter and not margarine)
2 eggs
1/3 cup of sugar (I've used Splenda, too, and it comes out great)

Directions:

Preheat oven to 375 degrees. Mix everything together and pour into a suitably sized dish. Bake for 1 hour. After the hour, test the center to check for doneness. (for me, I find it takes a little over an hour) It will be a very moist, casserole-like consistency. Served with a spoon, not cut with a knife.

Note: Enjoy! I'm always asked for the recipe after the meal is over. I hope your family finds it as delicious as mine does!

Mary Jo Putney
www.maryjoputney.com

Potato Kale Soup
(a Portuguese peasant soup, modified from a recipe run in the Baltimore Sun)

Ingredients:

This makes a very large batch—at least 16 servings, and requires a very large pot. You may prefer to halve ingredients. It helps to have a food processor for chopping the onions and garlic, and slicing the potatoes and kale. Saves a lot of time.

- 1 lb. hot Italian sausage, squeezed from casings, browned, and drained. (Or use chorizo sausage if you prefer—it's more authentic, but I like the bite of the Italian sausage.)
- 2 large onions, chopped
- 12 cloves of garlic, peeled and mashed
- 2 tbsp. olive oil
- 3 to 4 qts. chicken stock (7 cans of Campbells, diluted, or 3 big Swanson's 49 oz. cans)
- 4 lbs. of potatoes, sliced (if you use young, thin-skinned potatoes like Yukon Gold, they don't need to be peeled. If old and tough, peel them.)
- 1 1/2 lbs. of kale, approximately, washed, cleaned, and shredded. (Collard or mustard greens can be used, I'm told. And if you can buy washed and cut kale, all the better!) salt and pepper to taste (For this quantity, I use about a tbsp. of salt and a half tsp. of freshly ground pepper)

Directions:

Sautee onions and garlic in olive oil until translucent, 5 to 10 minutes.

Place all ingredients except the kale in a large soup pot, bring to a boil, then simmer until potatoes are tender and have started to break down. While it's simmering, you can wash the kale, strip out the tough stems, and send it through the slicer on the food processor.

When potatoes are tender and crumbling a bit, stir the chopped kale in and simmer for about 5 minutes more. Adjust seasoning and serve. Tastes good with corn bread, which is the traditional Portuguese way. Freezes well.

The original Sun recipe rated is at 254 calories a serving, but I make no guarantees for my version. Enjoy!

❖❖❖

Dianne Castell
www.DianneCastell.com

Two Minute Taco Soup

Ingredients & Directions:

In a big pot: brown 1 lb. ground beef with 1 chopped onion and taco season packet
Add 2 cans chopped tomatoes with garlic
Add 1 can each un-drained:
- hominy
- yellow corn
- black beans
- pinto beans

Simmer for as long as you have (smells great) Serve with dollop of sour cream and sprinkle of shredded cheddar

Author Note:

Perfect for fall!

Mary Jo Putney
www.maryjoputney.com

Tomato Lentil Soup

Ingredients:

2 tbsp. olive or vegetable oil
2 large onions, finely chopped (about 2 cups)
2 medium stalks of celery, cut in half inch pieces
4 cloves garlic, minced
4 medium carrots, chopped
2 qts. of water
1 lb. dried lentils, picked over and rinsed
8 tsp. chicken or vegetable bouillon
2 tsp. dried thyme
1/2 tsp. pepper
salt to taste (for this amount, perhaps 2 – 3 tsp.)
2 (28 oz.) cans of diced tomatoes, undrained

Optional:

8-16 oz. chopped smoked sausage or ham

Directions:

Sauté onion, celery, carrots, and garlic in oil for five minutes or so, until the vegetables soften.

Combine all ingredients except tomatoes; bring to a boil and simmer covered for 30-45 minutes or so until lentils and vegetables are tender. Add tomatoes, heat through and simmer for another 15 minutes or so. 16 or so servings. Tastes good with a dollop of plain yogurt or sour cream added just before serving.

Brenda Williamson
www.BrendaWilliamson.com

Potato Soup Supper

Ingredients:

12 medium potatoes, peeled & diced
2 celery ribs, sliced
1 large onion, diced
12 oz. evaporated milk
2 cups regular milk mixed with 4 heaping tbsp. cornstarch
4 cups frozen green peas
Lawry's Season Salt to taste
Black pepper to taste
1 lb. kielbasa, sliced & cooked or 1 lb. cubed baked ham.

Directions:

Cook potatoes, celery, & onion in 5 quart pot on top of stove with water just level over potatoes. Once potatoes are tender, add everything else and simmer until thickened.

Jules Bennett
www.julesbennett.com

Sour Cream Corn Bread

Ingredients & Directions:

8 oz. sour cream
1 egg
8 oz. self-rising corn meal mix
1/4 cup oil
1/4 cup sugar

Mix together.

Bake at 350 degrees for 30 minutes or until golden brown.

Vina Foster, Lori Foster's mother in law

Mexican Cornbread

Ingredients & Directions:

1 1/2 cups cornmeal
1 (15 oz.) can cream style corn
1 can chopped green chilies
1 cup cheddar cheese, shredded
1/2 cup vegetable oil
1/2 cup milk
1 egg

Preheat oven to 400 degrees. Mix all ingredients and then put into a lightly greased cast iron skillet.

Bake 30 to 35 minutes or until lightly browned on top.

Jules Bennett
www.julesbennett.com

Monkey Bread

Ingredients & Directions:

2 large or 4 small cans of biscuits.
Cut each biscuit into 4 pieces.
Put into a bag: 3/4 cup of white sugar and 1 tbsp. of cinnamon.
Shake biscuits in the bag (a few at a time) then place in greased bundt or angel food pan.

Topping:
1 cup brown sugar
3/4 cup oleo
1 tbsp. cinnamon.

Bring to boil; then pour over the biscuits.
Bake at 350 degrees for about 45 minutes.
Nuts optional.

Susan Andersen
www.susanandersen.com

Tortellini Soup

Ingredients:

1/2 cup finely chopped onion
1/2 cup finely chopped celery
1/2 cup finely chopped green bell pepper
2 cloves garlic, minced
2 tbsp. all-purpose flour
2 cans vegetable broth
15 oz. (1 can) tomato sauce
14 1/2 oz. (1 can) diced tomatoes
1 cup tortellini (NOTE: the original recipe called for them uncooked but I learned the hard way this sucks up too much of the liquids)
1/2 tsp. each: oregano, basil, & sage
1/2 tsp. each: pepper & sugar
2 tsp. parsley

Directions:

Sauté first 4 ingredients in a little olive oil until soft. Stir in flour. Slowly add vegetable broth, stirring constantly; bring to a boil. Add remaining ingredients and simmer 15 minutes.

Note: I'm a fool for Cross country skiing. Classic or Skate, it doesn't matter to me, as long as I can be out on the snow where it's quiet and pretty. After a day on the trails or in the woods, nothing hits the spot like a bowl of soup. This is one of my favorites.

Spice up your night with a hot bowl of Susan Andersen's Tortellini Soup.

Patricia Sargeant
www.patriciasargeant.com

Chicken Noodle Soup
Quick (20 minutes) and easy (six ingredients)

Ingredients:

4 cups chicken broth
Ground black pepper
1 sliced carrot
1 chopped celery
1 potato
1 jalapeno pepper (I like spicy foods <g>)
1 onion
Mushrooms, egg noodles, already-cooked chicken to taste

Directions:

Sauté mushrooms and jalapeno pepper in pan. Boil broth, pepper, carrot, celery, potato, and onion in saucepan. Add mushrooms, jalapeno pepper, noodles and chicken. Heat for 10 minutes (or until the noodles are done).

Bon appétit!

Donna MacMeans
www.DonnaMacMeans.com

Italian Sausage Soup

My family loves this entree soup, especially when served with a nice loaf of a good crusty bread and a salad. It warms you through and through so we save it for fall and winter. It's a soup that is even better the second day.

Ingredients:

1 lb. Italian Sausage
1 cup coarsely chopped onion
2-3 cloves of garlic (although I use the bottled stuff)
5 cups beef broth
1/2 cup water
1/2 red wine
1 (28 oz.) can tomatoes & juice (stewed, diced, whatever)
1 (15 oz.) can tomato sauce
1 tsp. basil
1 tsp. oregano
1 1/2 cup sliced carrots (I use a small bag of baby carrots)
1 1/2 cup sliced zucchini
1 medium green pepper, chopped
grated parmesan cheese
medium shell pasta

Directions:

Brown the sausage along with the onion and garlic.

Put in a large pot and add beef broth, water, red wine, tomatoes, tomato sauce, basil and oregano. Bring to a boil then simmer for 45 minutes. Add carrots, zucchini, and green pepper and simmer another 45 minutes. Cook the pasta as directed on the package.

To serve: put some cooked pasta in the bowl, ladle in soup, top with parmesan cheese.

Justine Wittich
www.cofw.org/TinaWittich.html

Sour Cherry Salad

Ingredients & Directions:

1 can sour cherries (buy in the pie filling section)
2/3 cup sugar
1/3 cup water
Large (double) pkg. of cherry Jello
1 (8 oz.) bottle of Coke
1 can crushed pineapple (do not drain)
1/2 cup or more broken pecans or walnuts

Combine cherries, sugar and water in saucepan and bring to boil. Remove from heat, add box of cherry gelatin and let cool. Add Coke, pineapple and nuts. Refrigerate.

Amanda McIntyre
www.amandamcintyre.net

Taffy Apple Salad

Ingredients& Directions:

16-20 oz. Crushed Pineapple (drained)
3 Granny Smith Apples (cut in bite-size chunks with skin)
2-3 handfuls of salted Spanish peanuts
3 King-size Snickers Bars (cut into bite-size chunks)
Medium container of Cool Whip topping

Fold ingredients together shortly before serving. Will last about a day in refrigerator, use a bit of lemon juice.

Great for potlucks!

Carys Weldon
www.carysweldon.com

Dump Soup

Ingredients & Directions:

I have a large family, lots of kids. When there are leftovers, there isn't much. A couple spoonfuls here and there. Usually, we fed them to the dogs. After all, there wasn't enough of any one dish on the table to serve a crowd another meal. I know, it sounds wasteful, and it was. Made the dogs happy, though.

We heard about DUMP SOUP at a church potluck and, frankly, the concept scared us. Dump leftovers in a pot, add some water, call it soup. Aaaggghhh. My kids were horrified. Visions of people scooping unknown dishes from the bowels of the fridge came to mind. Sniff and dump. "Looks okay to me."

You can see why this did not appeal to us. But, a friend of ours said, "The secret to making good Dump Soup is not to keep things in the fridge."

So, that sort of horrified me more. "If not the fridge, where would you keep these leftovers?"

"In a freezer proof container in the freezer, silly. Surely, you have leftover corn and beans and other veggies sometimes. Maybe some meat but," she glanced around me, looking at my brood. "I know you don't have enough leftovers to feed that army twice from one meal."

"Let me get this straight," I said. "You take little scoops of stuff and put it into, say, a Tupperware container?"

She corrected me. "I use Rubbermaid."

Another lady chimed in. "I use Glad disposables. You just drop the stuff in as it comes. Once a week, or whenever it gets full, we set it in a bowl of warm water for a few minutes, then it plops right out into a crock pot or stew pot. You put a lid on it and let it simmer until melted and warm."

The first friend said, "Sometimes I add a can of regular soup, or broth, and when I'm really broke, I just go for some water and a small can of tomato paste. Mix it up and let it simmer."

"But, what about seasonings?" I had to ask. We don't like blah food around my house. My husband's Italian. The kids are chips off his block.

"Oh. Easy. Each time you make corn, you salt and pepper it, right? And green beans...what do you put in that?"

"I don't know. Sometimes salt, pepper, butter. Sometimes bacon and onions. Depends."

"Right. So, all that has seasoning in it. I'm telling you, you should try it."

Well, I certainly wasn't going to try someone else's Dump Soup. Call me picky. But, I did try it. And, lo and behold, we liked it. It's the best thing to pull out, pop in a crockpot for Sunday dinner, or another day when you are on the run. And, if you find that it has no meat in it, you can simply open a can of chicken, or beef, and drop it in.

To plump it up, sometimes, I take frozen or dehydrated, diced potatoes—like hash browns—and pour them in, too. It's great.

Amanda McIntyre
www.amandamcintyre.net

Yummy Coleslaw

Ingredients:

2 pkgs. ready made coleslaw mix
2 bunches of green onion
Small bag sunflower seeds
Small bag slivered almonds
2 pkgs. of Beef Ramen noodles (uncooked)
*Reserve seasoning packet form Ramen for dressing

Directions:

Place all ingredients in a large bowl, crush dry Ramen
noodles and add to mixture

Just before serving, mix dressing:

Blend with whisk-
Beef season packet from Ramen noodles
1 cup of vegetable oil
1/2 cup sugar
Pour over mixture and toss
Variations: add white raisins or drained can of Mandarin
orange slices to the mix
1/3 cup of vinegar

Susanne Marie Knight
www.susanneknight.com

Desert-Island Style Crab Salad

Ingredients:

1 package (1 lb.) imitation crab meat, flaked
1/2 cup sweet onion, chopped
1/2 cup celery, chopped
1/4 cup sour cream
1 1/2 cup mayonnaise
2/3 cup Italian salad dressing
2 tsp. lemon juice
Salt and pepper to taste

Directions:

Combine crab meat, onion, and celery in large bowl. Mix remaining ingredients in a separate bowl, then pour mixture over crab meat. Toss lightly, then refrigerate before serving.

Author Note: In my paranormal romantic suspense THE COMING, Jack and his men have a variety of food on their *paradise* desert island, and often assembled the fixings for a desert island-style salad. Here's a tasty recipe they might have whipped up using nature's bounty.

Nicole Jordan
www.NicoleJordanAuthor.com

Low-fat Banana Nut Bread

Ingredients:

1 3/4 cups flour
3 tsp. baking powder
1/2 tsp. salt
1/4 cup applesauce
1/3 cup sugar
2 eggs
4 large ripe bananas
3/4 cup chopped pecans (optional)

Directions:

Mash bananas in medium mixing bowl (microwaving for 2-3 minutes first makes them soft, but cool a little before adding to other ingredients).

In large mixing bowl mix eggs, sugar, and applesauce. In large measuring cup mix flour, salt and baking powder.

Add flour mix to egg mix and beat at medium speed for 1 minute. Add bananas and beat at low speed for 30 seconds. Add nuts and stir by hand until evenly mixed.

Pour into 2 buttered loaf pans and bake at 350 degrees for about 45 minutes. (Or for a larger loaf, use 1 buttered loaf pan and bake for about 55 minutes.) Comes out very moist and flavorful!

Patricia Lorenz
www.PatriciaLorenz.com

Pea Salad

Ingredients:

6-7 hard boiled eggs (put in frig overnight before dicing)
1 cup sharp cheddar cheese cut in small cubes
1 cup chopped celery
1 large red onion chopped fine
1 pkg. of frozen baby peas

Directions:

Mix all ingredients and stir with Marzetti's coleslaw dressing to taste.

Note:

Patricia Lorenz is an internationally-known inspirational, art-of-living writer and speaker. Patricia is the country's top contributor to the Chicken Soup for the Soul books with stories in over 30 of the Chicken Soup books so far. She's had over 400 articles published in numerous magazines and newspapers; is a contributing writer for sixteen Daily Guideposts books and three dozen anthologies; and is an award-winning newspaper columnist.

Patricia Lorenz
www.PatriciaLorenz.com

Crab Slaw

Ingredients & Directions:

Mix together:

Broccoli slaw mix (comes in bags in produce section)
1 bunch green onions sliced
1 lb. crab salad from deli (cut up crab if it's in huge pieces)
1 cup slivered almonds
1 pkg. chicken Ramen crushed

Dressing:

1/2 cup oil
1/4 cup white vinegar
Ramen seasoning packet
3-4 tbsp. sugar

Mix and pour over salad just before serving.

Note:

Patricia Lorenz is an internationally-known inspirational, art-of-living writer and speaker. Patricia is the country's top contributor to the Chicken Soup for the Soul books with stories in over 30 of the Chicken Soup books so far. She's had over 400 articles published in numerous magazines and newspapers; is a contributing writer for sixteen Daily Guideposts books and three dozen anthologies; and is an award-winning newspaper columnist.

Patricia Lorenz
www.PatriciaLorenz.com

Raspberry Salad

Ingredients:

1 large box raspberry Jello
2 cups boiling water to dissolve Jello
1 cup or half-a-25-ounce jar of applesauce
1 tea cinnamon

Directions:

Refrigerate

When Jello is semi-hardened beat in one small container of cool whip

Add 1-2 packages frozen raspberries, stir and pour into fancy dishes

Refrigerate

Note:

Patricia Lorenz is an internationally-known inspirational, art-of-living writer and speaker. Patricia is the country's top contributor to the Chicken Soup for the Soul books with stories in over 30 of the Chicken Soup books so far. She's had over 400 articles published in numerous magazines and newspapers; is a contributing writer for sixteen Daily Guideposts books and three dozen anthologies; and is an award-winning newspaper columnist.

Michele Stegman
www.Asylett.com

Vegetarian Adventure Soup

Ingredients:

4 cups water - boil, then add 1 cup texturized vegetable protein (widely available)
Add 1/4 to 1/2 cup chopped onions that have been sautéed in chicken bouillon.
Add chopped green pepper
Add 1 can diced tomatoes w/oregano and basil flavoring
Add 1 can pinto beans
Add 1 can black beans
1/2 to 3/4 cup frozen corn
Optional—add squash, potatoes, carrots

Seasonings: cayenne pepper, minced garlic, cumin, oregano, basil, sage, parsley, celery seed.

Directions:

Simmer until everything is done. You may have to add more water.

Serve over spaghetti or with corn bread

Author Note:

This soup is for those who don't use recipes when they cook. It's one of those "add a bit of this and a little of that" recipes. There were no amounts given for many of the ingredients when I got the recipe and my soup turned out differently than the person's I got it from and yours will be different yet.

Michele Stegman
www.Asylett.com

Corn Bread

Ingredients:

1 1/4 cup flour
3/4 cup white corn meal
Heaping tbsp. sugar
Dash of salt
3 tsp. baking powder
1/2 tsp. baking soda
1 egg
Scant 1/4 cup vegetable oil
1 1/2 to 2 cups buttermilk, enough to make the batter
    pourable, not thin, but not so thick that you have to pat
    it into the edges of the pan.

Directions:

Put about 2 tbsp. butter flavor Crisco into a cast iron skillet
and put it in the oven while the oven heats to 425 degrees. Mix
dry ingredients. Add rest of ingredients, mix just until blended
but don't beat. Pour the batter into the hot skillet and bake
about 25 to 30 minutes. Immediately dump out onto a plate.

Author Note:

Corn bread is part of my heritage. I grew up on it. I've
experimented with the recipe and this is what works for me.
Corn bread can be made in muffin pans, as pancakes on top of
the stove when you are in a hurry, or in a glass cake pan. But
the very best corn bread just has to be made in a hot cast iron
skillet.

Jim Alexander
www.speculativefictionreview.com/
MainFrame.asp?BookName=BlamGame&CookEn=true

Leonardo da Vinci's Chickpea Soup
(from Famous Vegetarians and their favorite recipes, by Rynn Berry)

Serves 8.

Ingredients:

1 cup chickpeas
1/2 oz. flour
1 tsp. oil
1 tsp. salt
20 grains crushed peppercorn
1 tbsp. cinnamon
3 pints water
2 tsp. sage
2 tsp. rosemary
2 tbsp. chopped parsley
Dash of onion powder

Directions:

Process the chickpeas until smooth. Add this to the water and spices in a large saucepan. Add the flour and mix. Bring to a rolling boil. Reduce heat when soup thickens.

Susan Elizabeth Phillips
www.susanephillips.com

THIS HEART OF MINE Harvest Soup

Ingredients:

2 Cans (4 Cups) Chicken or Vegetarian Broth (The boys weren't home, so I used College Inn's Low Fat)
4 or 5 medium-to-small Sweet Potatoes
2 Cinnamon Sticks
Thyme to taste
About 1/4 cup Peanut Butter

Directions:

Peel and cut up uncooked sweet potatoes. Cook in saucepan with 1 1/2 cans of the broth, the cinnamon sticks, and thyme. (Use thyme to taste. Maybe a 1/2 to 1 tsp. dry. I was using fresh from my garden and just threw in a handful.) Simmer until the sweet potato is mooshy. Pull out cinnamon sticks and pour sweet potato mixture into food processor. Process until blended in. Add extra broth for desired thickness. (I like it pretty thick.) Add peanut butter to taste. Return to stove and reheat. Serve with a nice salad and enjoy. (Even the Calebow kids like this one!)

Note:

I think Phoebe Calebow, Molly Somerville's big sister, would love serving this to Dan and the kids. Warning! I didn't measure anything while I was making this, so these directions are a little whifty! I served 4 people with this quantity.

Bianca D'Arc
www.biancadarc.com

Potato Leek Soup with Truffle Oil

Ingredients:

Approximately 1 lb. of fresh leek
2-3 medium potatoes
1-2 tbsp. butter
Water
Truffle Oil

Directions:

Cut leeks into small pieces and wash thoroughly. (If you don't get all the dirt out, you will have crunchy soup!) Peel and cut up the potatoes into small pieces and set aside.

In a large soup pot, melt the butter until it sizzles. Add the cut leeks and sauté for a few minutes until the leek begins to wilt. Add several cups of water. I usually eyeball the amount. For thinner soup, add more water, for thicker soup, use less. Add potatoes and bring to a boil, then let simmer for an hour or so, stirring occasionally. The soup should thicken a bit, depending on how much water you put in. A little trick – leave the pot lid off to evaporate some of the water if you want your soup to be thicker.

Dish up bowls of the soup and as a final garnish, add a dollop of truffle oil—about a tbsp.—to the center of each bowl. When you serve it, the oil will most likely float on top, but as you eat, the lovely taste of the oil will blend in with the leeks for an unforgettable flavor. And it smells divine!

Note: This is a simple recipe, but incredibly delicious. I was inspired by the potato leek soup served at my favorite little Irish restaurant across from Penn Station in New York City. The restaurant is called *Tir Na Nog*, which is Gaelic for Land of Eternal Youth. Their soup is pureed with no chunks, but I like my soup to have some substance, so I combined an old family recipe for hearty potato leek soup with the delectable garnish of truffle oil that they use at *Tir Na Nog* to give the soup an incredible, rich flavor. Enjoy!

Jo Leigh
www.joleigh.com

Macadamia Nut Fruit Salad

Ingredients:

8 oz. cream cheese
1 cup Macadamia nuts, chopped
2 medium cartons of Cool Whip (8 oz. each)
1 small can Mandarin oranges
1 small envelope unflavored gelatin
1 medium can chunky fruit
1 medium can fruit cocktail
2/3 cup mayonnaise
1 tbsp. lemon juice
1/2 cup sugar

Directions:

Cream sugar, mayonnaise, cream cheese and lemon juice. Heat 1/2 cup fruit juice to dissolve gelatin. Cool. Add macadamia nuts, fruits to cream cheese mixture. Add gelatin and one carton of cool whip. Refrigerate for at least one hour. One hour before serving, add second carton of cool whip.

Lisa Freeman - Reader
"Made with Italian Sausage, this soup is just as
spicy as a Lori Foster story."

Sausage and Potato Soup

Ingredients:

1 lb. sausage (mild or Italian)
2 large Russet baking potatoes, washed thoroughly cut in
half, then in 1/4 inch slices
2 cans chicken broth
1 pint water
1 onion, chopped or equivalent onion powder
1/2 can/pkg. Oscar Meyer Real Bacon Bits
1 cup heavy whipping cream
2 cups Kale or Swiss Chard, chopped (this is optional)

Directions:

Brown sausage; set aside to drain. In large boiler, combine
potatoes, broth, water and onion. Cook until potatoes are done.
Add sausage, bacon, salt and pepper to taste, and simmer for
another 10 minutes. Turn to low heat, add Kale and cream.
Heat through and serve.

Melissa Schroeder
www.melissaschroeder.net

Grandma Bodnar's Nut Rolls

Ingredients:

Dough:
1 cup lukewarm milk
2 eggs
3 envelopes yeast
1/2 cup butter
1/4 cup sugar
1 tsp. salt
4 cups flour

Filling (mix together):
1-1/2 cup walnuts or pecans
1 cup sugar
1 tsp. vanilla
1/2 cup milk
1 egg white

Directions:

Preheat the oven to 350 degrees. Crumble yeast into warm milk. Add to rest of dough ingredients and mix well until hands are clean from dough. Let rise 1 hour in a warm place. Roll out to about 1/4 inch thick and spread with filling, not too close to edge. Roll up and seal all edges so filling doesn't leak out. Let rise 1 hour again. Bake and brush with butter. Bake in a preheated oven for 30 minutes.

Author Note:

This recipe is a family tradition for the Bodnars, my mother and father. It comes from my father's Czechoslovakian grandmother, and my grandmother and mother have carried on the tradition. I spent many Christmas breaks forced into child labor making these. Christmas isn't the same if I don't have a piece of this with a smear of butter and a cup of coffee.

Lisa Freeman - Reader
"As sweet as an afternoon spent with a Dianne Castell book."

Orange Mountain Salad

Ingredients & Directions:

16 oz. cottage cheese
20 oz. crushed pineapple, drain thoroughly
1 pkg. large orange Jello
9 oz. whipped topping
2 cans drained mandarin oranges, drain thoroughly
1 cup chopped nuts, optional

Mix Jello and cottage cheese. Add rest of ingredients and mix thoroughly. Put in glass dish and chill.

Christine Feehan
www.christinefeehan.com

Jello Salad

Ingredients:

2 large boxes of strawberry/banana Jello
2 cups fresh strawberries
2 cups fresh sliced bananas
1 tub Cool Whip

Directions:

Make Jello as directed, and then let cool. When slightly gelled, fold in cool whip first then fold in fruit. Chill in refrigerator, and serve when Jello is firm.

Amber Green
www.shapeshiftersinlust.com

Creamy Onion Soup

Ingredients:

5 or 6 strong yellow onions
1/2 to 1 stick salted (yellow-box) butter (start with
1/2 stick and add more if your pan needs it)
1 tbsp. flour (or half as much rice powder or cornstarch)
2 shot glasses dense meat drippings, jelly, or demi-glace
2 fist-sized leftover boiled/steamed potatoes (or three
smaller ones) or equivalent amount of leftover mashed
potatoes (Golden potatoes are lovely)
1 can evaporated (not sweetened condensed) milk
A little more milk, fresh or canned
Salt and pepper

Directions:

You need a food processor or a ricer for this.

Mince the onions and rice or mash the potatoes. Sauté'
minced onions in butter, then rice or puree them. Return onion
mush to pan. Sprinkle in flour, then meat jelly. Stir in potatoes.
Bring the puree to the right consistency with milk and simmer,
stirring, for a few minutes until everything is good and hot. Salt
and pepper very lightly, then taste to see if you need more.

Michelle M. Pillow
www.michellepillow.com

Dan's Tomato Basil Soup

Ingredients:

2 cans Peeled Tomatoes (chopped) or 4-5 tomatoes peeled,
    seeded and diced
4 cups tomato juice
14 leaves fresh basil
1 block (8 ounces) cream cheese melted
1/2 cup butter
1/4 cup minced garlic
Salt, pepper to taste

Directions:

Simmer tomatoes and juice in over medium heat for 30 minutes. Optional- Puree the tomato mixture along with the basil leaves, and return the puree to the pot.

Place over medium heat, and stir in the cream cheese, butter and minced garlic.

Season to taste with spices.

Heat, stirring until the butter has melted. Do not boil.

Author Note:

Yields about 4-5 servings. My chef husband is forced to make this every year for family Christmas and it has become a holiday tradition in our household. It's very rich, but well worth the extra calories!

Brenda Novak
www.brendanovak.com

Pumpkin Bread

Ingredients:

4 eggs (beaten)
3 cup sugar
2 cup pumpkin
2/3 cup water
1 cup vegetable oil
3 1/2 cup flour
1/2 tsp. baking powder
2 tsp. baking soda
1 1/2 tsp. salt
3 tsp. cloves
3 tsp. nutmeg
3 tsp. cinnamon

Directions:

Mix all ingredients with beaters. Grease and flour pans (makes four small loaves or one large one). Bake at 325 for 1 1/4—1 1/2 hours.

Jo Dartlon
www.DartlonDesigns.com
affordable graphic and website designs

Dartlon Family version of Zuppa Toscana (or Italian potato soup)

Ingredients:

1-1 1/2 lb. ground hot Italian sausage
1/4 cup bacon or Prosciutto
2 tsp. crushed red peppers
1 large diced onion
2 cloves of diced garlic
2 diced carrots
1/2 tsp. Tony's seasoning (if you prefer less heat, you
    should leave out the Tony's :)
8 cups of chicken broth
4-5 large sliced Russet potatoes (skins on)
Salt and fresh ground pepper to taste
1 cup heavy cream
1/4 cup fresh parsley
8 oz. package of shredded Italian cheese

Sautee Italian sausage, bacon, crushed red pepper, onion, garlic and carrot in pot. Drain. (if you want a thicker soup, now is the time to add some flour and create a roux.)

Add chicken broth and 1/2 tsp Tony's to the pot. Cook until boiling.

Add potatoes, salt and pepper and cook until soft (about half an hour.)

Add heavy cream and parsley and cook until thoroughly heated. (don't overcook. The heavy cream can scorch easily.)

Sprinkle with Italian cheese. Yum!!

Note: This is an Italian soup that my 14 year old daughter and I came up with after trying to guess what all was in the Zuppa Toscana soup at Olive Garden. (we added a few extras that we thought made it even better, though.) Now we can't eat out without trying to guess all of the ingredients in our favorite dishes and recreating our own version at home.

Jodi Shadden - Reader

"These are super easy biscuits to make when you're busy reading your favorite Dianne Castell book!"

Drop Biscuits

Ingredients:

2 cups flour
1 tbsp. baking powder
1 tsp. salt
1/3 cup shortening
1 cup milk

Directions:

Pre-Heat oven to 450 degrees.

Sift together flour, salt, and baking powder. Cut in shortening until mixture looks like coarse meal. Make a hole in the center of the mixture and pour milk in. Stir until dry ingredients are damp. Drop by spoonful onto ungreased cookie sheet.

Bake 12-15 minutes.

Gemma Bruce
www.gemmabruce.com

Southern Cheese Sausage Biscuits

Ingredients:

2 1/4 cups Bisquick
1/2 cup milk
I cup shredded sharp cheese
I cup crumbled bulk sausage

Directions:

Brown sausage, crumbling it into fine pieces, when fully cooked set on a paper towel to drain.

Mix Bisquick, milk and cheese.

When thoroughly mixed, add cooled sausage.

You can adjust the amount of Bisquick depending on whether you want drop or rolled biscuits. Dropped biscuit dough is sticky to the touch. Drop a heaping tbsp. amount onto an ungreased cookie sheet, leaving room for biscuits to expand.

For rolled biscuits, add enough Bisquick to make the mixture easy to handle. Place on a floured board and knead 10-15 times (over kneading will make biscuits tough). Roll to desired height, cut with a floured biscuit cutter or jelly jar and place on an ungreased cookie sheet two inches apart.

Bake at 375 degrees from 10 to 15 minutes or until golden brown.

Great with soups or can be shaped smaller for the party tray.

Author Note: My grandmother use to make these from scratch. I've substituted Bisquick for a faster prep time.

J.C. Wilder / Dominique Adair
www.jcwilder.com / www.dominiqueadair.com

Asian Pasta Salad

Ingredients:

1 (16 ounce) package pasta
2 cups broccoli florets
1 red bell pepper, chopped
1/2 cup diced red onion
1 cup snow peas
1 cup Asian-style salad dressing
Salt to taste
Ground black pepper to taste
1 tbsp. minced fresh ginger root (optional)
1 tbsp. minced garlic (optional)
1 tbsp. sesame oil
1/2 tbsp. sesame seeds

Directions:

Blanch broccoli in rapidly boiling water for 3 to 5 minutes. Drain. Blanch snow peas for 1 to 2 minutes then drain.

Cook one pound of pasta in a large pan of boiling water until al dente. Drain, and transfer to a large bowl.

Toss pasta with salad dressing. Toss with broccoli, red pepper, red onion, and snow peas, ginger, and garlic. Season with salt and pepper to taste.

Refrigerate for several hours or overnight. When serving, sprinkle with sesame oil and sesame seeds.

Lisa Freeman - Reader

This soup is guaranteed to keep the family happy while you read your newest Lucy Monroe book.

Sausage and Potato Soup

Ingredients:

1 lb. sausage (mild or Italian)
2 large Russet baking potatoes, washed thoroughly cut in half, then in 1/4 inch slices
2 cans chicken broth
1 quart water
1 onion, chopped or equivalent onion powder
1/2 can Oscar Meyer Real Bacon Bits
1 cup heavy whipping cream
2 cups Kale or Swiss Chard, chopped (this is optional)

Directions:

Brown sausage; set aside to drain. In large boiler, combine potatoes, broth, water and onion. Cook until potatoes are done. Add sausage, bacon, salt and pepper to taste, and simmer for another 10 minutes. Turn to low heat, add Kale and cream. Heat through and serve.

Lisa Freeman - Reader

Easy to make, so you can get back to your favorite
Toni Blake book.

Orange Mountain Salad

Ingredients:

16 oz. cottage cheese
20 oz. crushed pineapple, drain thoroughly
1 pkg. large orange Jello
9 oz. whipped topping
2 cans drained mandarin oranges, drain thoroughly
1 cup chopped nuts, optional

Directions:

Mix Jello and cottage cheese. Add rest of ingredients and
mix thoroughly. Put in glass dish and chill.

Janice Maynard

www.janicemaynard.com

Orange "Dump" Salad

Ingredients & Directions:

In bottom of bowl (I use a large Tupperware bowl with lid)
put 12 ounces of cottage cheese. Pour one small package of
orange Jello (dry) on top of cottage cheese. In a colander, drain
a 15-16 ounce can of crushed pineapple and one 11 ounce can
of mandarin oranges. Get out as much juice as possible, then
add fruit to Jello and cottage cheese. Finally, add one 8 ounce
sour cream and an 8 ounce cool whip. Mix well... refrigerate at
least two hours. I like to make it the day before.

Cryna Palmiere - Reader

I usually serve this with coffee if I have company, and then we eat while we talk about our favorite new romance novels.

Johnny Cake

Ingredients:

1 cup flour
2 tsp. baking powder
1/4 tsp. salt
1 cup corn meal
1/4 cup sugar
1 egg
1 cup milk
Piece of butter/margarine the size of an egg

Directions:

Sift flour and baking powder together, add cornmeal and sugar. Melt butter and add to well beaten egg, add to the other ingredients along with the milk. Beat all together lightly.

Grease a 9x9 cake pan. Pour in batter and bake at 375 degrees for 30 to 40 minutes, or until done depending on your stove.

Vegetables

Jamie Denton
www.jamiedenton.net

Artichokes AuGratin
(Side Dish)

Ingredients:

2 (14 oz.) cans water-packed artichoke hearts, drained & quartered
1 garlic clove, minced
1/4 cup (unsalted) butter, divided
2 tbsp. flour
1/2 tsp. salt
1/4 tsp. pepper
1-1/2 cups milk
1 egg, lightly beaten
1/2 cup shredded Swiss cheese 1 tbsp. dry bread crumbs
1/8 tsp. paprika

Directions:

In a skillet, sauté the artichokes and garlic in 2 tbsp. of butter until tender. Transfer to a greased 1-quart baking dish.

In a saucepan, melt the remaining butter. Stir in flour, salt and pepper until smooth. Gradually add milk. Bring to a boil; cook and stir for 2 minutes until thickened. Remove from heat. Stir in a small amount of hot mixture into egg; return all to pan, stirring constantly. Stir in 1/4 cup cheese until melted.

Pour over artichokes; sprinkle with remaining cheese. Combine crumbs and paprika; sprinkle over top. Bake, uncovered, at 400 degrees for 20-25 minutes.

Yield: 4-6 servings.

Lori Foster
www.lorifoster.com

Fried Zucchini

Ingredients:

1 large, ripe zucchini
1/4 cup corn meal
1 tsp. salt
1 tsp. pepper
1/4 cup flour
1 egg, stirred in bowl
Oil

Directions:

Cut zucchini into thick slices.
Mix corn meal, flour, pepper and salt together.
Dip zucchini slices into egg mixture, then flour/corn meal mixture.
Fry in heated oil, on medium high heat, until lightly browned on both sides.

Author Note: This same recipe can used on Okra, or Green Tomatoes

Vina Foster, Lori Foster's mother in law

Cheddar Scalloped Potatoes

Ingredients:

2 tbsp. margarine
1 small onion, sliced
1 can Campbell's Broccoli Cheese soup
1/2 cup milk
1/4 tsp. pepper
4 medium potations, cooked and sliced (about 3 1/2 cup)

Directions:

In skillet over medium heat, in hot margarine, cook onion until tender.

Stir in soup, milk, and pepper. Heat to boiling. Add potatoes.

Reduce heat to low.

Cover; simmer 5 minutes or until hot and bubbling, stirring occasionally.

Garnish with sage if desired.

Susanne Marie Knight
www.susanneknight.com

Brokenhearted Broccoli or Broccoli Bake

Ingredients:

2 (10 oz.) frozen broccoli spears
dashes of salt and pepper
6 slices tomato
2 tbsp. butter
11 oz. can condensed cheese soup
1 tbsp. lemon juice

Directions:

Cook broccoli as directed until almost tender.
Drain.
Arrange in 10 x 6 baking dish and sprinkle with salt and pepper.
Place tomato slices along outside edge and sprinkle with salt and pepper.
Dot broccoli with butter.
Blend soup and juice until smooth, then pour over broccoli.
Bake at 350 degrees for 20 minutes.

Note:

In my Regency THE RELUCTANT LANDLORD, at the dinner table, Katrina brokenheartedly concentrates on her broccoli spear because she fears Quentin is still interested in Therese. Here's an easy and delicious recipe to keep your attention on this healthy vegetable as well!

Brenda Williamson
www.BrendaWilliamson.com

Fried Green Tomatoes

Ingredients:

4 green tomatoes, sliced 1/4 inch
Salt, pepper, to taste
1 cup yellow cornmeal
1 cup flour

Directions:

Mix cornmeal, flour, salt & pepper together.
Coat both sides of your tomato slices in the mixture and sauté over medium heat in a little oil in a frying pan until brown.

Author Note:

For a spicy flavor, add a pinch of cayenne pepper to the coating mixture.

Lori Foster
www.lorifoster.com

Easy Cheesy Potatoes

Ingredients:

4 large potatoes
Velveeta Cheese
Butter
Salt

Directions:

Boil the potatoes, and then peel the skins away.

Slice them into a microwave proof bowl, alternating layers of potatoes, Velveeta Cheese, thin slices of butter and a sprinkling of salt.

Microwave on high for 3 minutes, or until cheese is melted. Voila! Very tasty, and good with Sloppy Joes, hamburgers, or any meat off the grill.

Author Note:

When I came home from the hospital after having my third son, a wonderful neighbor (I still miss her!) brought over a pot of sloppy Joe mix and buns, a 2 liter of cola, and a dish of these potatoes. It was such a surprise, and so thoughtful.

J.C. Wilder / Dominique Adair
www.jcwilder.com / www.dominiqueadair.com

Vegetable Feta Medley

Ingredients:

1 1/2 cups uncooked long-grain white rice
3 cups water
1/2 cup chopped red onion
1 cup chopped celery
1 cup chopped cucumber
4 oz. feta cheese
1 tbsp. olive oil
2 tbsp. red wine vinegar

Directions:

Place rice and water in a medium-size pot. Bring water to a boil, when boiled reduce heat to a simmer, cover pot and let rice cook until tender.

In a large mixing bowl, combine red onion, celery, and cucumber. Crumble the feta into the bowl. Cover the vegetable mixture with cooked rice, cover and let sit for 5 minutes.

Toss vegetable and feta with oil and vinegar, and serve.

Author Note:

Very simple recipe—great for the summer. You can save time by cooking the rice in the microwave (if you have a rice cooker) and I usually add more feta because I love the stuff. You can use flavored feta such as the basil or sun dried tomato ones for a little extra kick. This is also good served cold (the next day) with grilled chicken—YUM!

Ellie Davis – Lori Foster's stepmother
"I enjoy eating this with or without a hot dog while
reading about the CINCINNATI REDS."

German Potato Salad

Ingredients:

6 slices BACON, cut into small pieces and fried until well
done.
Stir in 1/4 cup FLOUR.
Add 1 cup VINEGAR, 1 1/2 cups WATER, and 1 1/2 cups
SUGAR.
Let simmer 20 minutes.

6 large potatoes
1 tsp. celery seed
Salt and pepper

Directions:

Boil Potatoes until tender. Peel and slice. Sprinkle with
salt, pepper, and celery seed. Pour simmered mixture over
potatoes and stir. Add 1/4 cup onions if desired. I personally
like to top with sliced hard-boiled eggs. Best served warm.

Jodi Shadden - Reader
"An easy side dish that won't take away from
your reading time!"

Laura's Beans

Ingredients:

2 cans pork-n-beans
1 can green beans, drained
1 can pinto beans, drained
1 can butter beans, drained
1 lb. bacon, diced
1 onion, diced
1/2 cup brown sugar
1 tbsp. Worcestershire sauce
3/4 cup ketchup

Directions:

Brown bacon and onion. Combine all ingredients in a crock
pot. Simmer until hot.

Note: Other beans may be added as desired.

Jayne Ann Krentz
www.jayneannkrentz.com

Roasted Garlic Spears & Asparagus Frank

Ingredients & Directions:

Rinse half a pound of garlic spears

Prep half a pound of asparagus by rinsing and snapping off woody ends of stems

Dry garlic spears and asparagus on paper towels. Toss asparagus and garlic spears with olive oil and salt and spread out on baking sheet. Roast at 350 degrees until asparagus is fork tender. Timing depends on thickness of asparagus. If you are using thick asparagus (or "fat grass" as they say down at the Market) give them a four minute head start in the oven before adding the garlic spears which are much thinner and will cook in about four or five minutes.

Note from Author: I have recently discovered some great new veggies. They are sold here in Seattle at the Pike Place Market as "Garlic Spears" and I'm probably the last person on the face of the earth to find them.

Garlic spears are the flower tops from Elephant Garlic and they are fabulous either alone or roasted together with asparagus. They don't actually taste much like garlic and don't leave the after taste (or the after breath, for that matter). They have become a great addition to the Frank Diet and they don't require any tofu!

Vina Foster – Lori Foster's mother in law

Bayou Red Beans and Rice

Ingredients:

1 lb. dried red kidney beans
1 hambone with 1 cut chopped ham
2 stalks celery with leaves, chopped
4 cups water
1 large onion, chopped
2 tsp. Tabasco sauce

Directions:

Soak beans overnight in water.
Pour into a large heavy pan or Dutch oven.
Add remaining ingredients.
Simmer 3 hours or until beans are tender.
Remove hambone, cut off meat and add to beans.

Add water when necessary during cooking. Water should barely cover beans at the end of the cooking time.
Remove 1 cup beans and mash to a paste (a blender maybe used).
Add back to remaining beans and stir until liquid is thickened.
Serve over hot rice.

Makes 8 1-cup servings.

Laurie Damron - Reader

You'll have time to read a couple of chapters in your favorite book while this bakes, and if you get carried away and it's in for a few minutes longer, no worries – it will be just fine!

Green Bean Casserole

Ingredients:

One large can green beans
2 tbsp. butter
1/2 tsp. salt
2 tbsp. Flour
1 cup stuffing mix
1 cup milk
1 tsp. butter
1/2 cup sharp cheddar cheese
1 tbsp. minced onion

Directions:

Drain green beans and turn into an 8" square baking dish. Melt 2 tbsp. butter, stir in flour, gradually add milk, cook and stir over medium heat until thickened. Stir in cheese, onion and salt and cook until cheese melts. Pour over beans, sprinkle with dry stuffing mix and dot with butter.

Bake at 350 degrees for 20-30 minutes.

Laurie Damron - Reader

These tasty potatoes will keep your family happy so you
can escape to do more reading on your favorite
Erin McCarthy novel.

Onion Roasted Potatoes

Ingredients:

1 envelope Lipton Onion Recipe Soup Mix
2 lbs. all-purpose potatoes, cut into large chunks
1/3 cup olive or vegetable oil (I use canola oil)

Directions:

Preheat oven to 450 degrees.

In large Ziploc bag, add all ingredients. Close bag and
shake until potatoes are evenly coated. Empty potatoes into
shallow baking or roasting pan; discard bag.

Bake, stirring occasionally, 40 minutes or until potatoes
are tender and golden brown.

Makes about 8 servings.

Laurie Damron - Reader

Perfect accompaniment to a summer dinner on the patio or deck. Put your feet up after and lose yourself in your favorite romance!

Fried Corn

Yield: 4 servings

Ingredients:

8 ears tender corn
1/4 cup bacon drippings
1 cup milk
Salt and pepper to taste
1 tsp. sugar (optional)
1 tbsp. butter

Directions:

Cut corn close to outer edge, then scrape the ear to remove all the milk. Add corn to bacon drippings which have been heated in heavy skillet. Add milk, salt, pepper and sugar. Stir often as corn burns easily.

Cook approximately 25-30 minutes, adding butter during the last few minutes of cooking.

Laurie Damron - Reader

A tasty side dish to complement a tasty novel by Dianne Castell.

Honey Glazed Carrots

Ingredients:

4 cups sliced carrots (1 lb.)
1/4 cup Kraft Balsamic Vinaigrette Dressing
2 tbsp. honey
2 tbsp. Planters chopped pecans

Bring carrots, dressing and honey to boil in saucepan.
Reduce heat to medium-low; cover. Simmer 15 min. or until tender.
Sprinkle with pecans.

Vina Foster, Lori Foster's mother in law

Broccoli Casserole

Ingredients:

2 pkgs. chopped broccoli
1 can creamed chicken soup
2 tbsp. lemon juice
1/4 cup mayonnaise
1/4 cup onion
2 eggs, beaten
1 cup sharp cheddar cheese, grated

Precook broccoli and sauté cook onion
Mix together soup, lemon juice, mayonnaise, onions, eggs and cheese.
Add to the broccoli and bake at 350 degrees for 30 minutes

Vina Foster, Lori Foster's mother in law

Broccoli Cheese Sauce

Ingredients:

1 can (10 3/4 oz.) Campbell's Broccoli cheese soup
1/3 cup milk

Directions:

Combine soup and milk
Over medium heat, heat until hot and bubbling, stirring often –
OR microwave, uncovered, on high for 5 minutes or until hot and bubbling, stirring halfway through heating.

Serve over vegetables such as broccoli, cauliflower and carrots.

Makes 1 1/2 cups

Gia Dawn
www.giadawn.com

In memory of my aunt, Beverly Hutton Shirley

Stuffed Eggplant

Ingredients:

1 large eggplant
1/2 cup water
1/2 tsp. salt
1 small can condensed cream of mushroom soup
1 tsp. Worcestershire sauce
1 cup Ritz crackers finely crumbled (about 24 crackers)
1/4 cup chopped onions
1 tbsp. butter
1 tbsp. chopped parsley
1 tbsp. butter or margarine
1 1/2 cups water

Directions:

Slice off one side of eggplant. Remove pulp to within 1/2 inch of skin. Heat 1/2 cup water and salt till boiling. Cook eggplant pulp in water until tender—about 10 minutes—and drain thoroughly. Cook onion in butter until tender but not brown. Add eggplant pulp, parsley, soup, Worcestershire sauce and cracker crumbs—reserving two tablespoons.

Fill eggplant shell with mixture. Place in a 10x6x11 1/2 inch baking dish, dot with one tbsp. butter and remaining cracker crumbs. Carefully pour 1 1/2 cups water in bottom of dish and bake in moderate oven 375 degrees until heated through. Serves 4-6.

Author Note:

I loved this as a girl, she always made it whenever we came to visit. Her son, Kevin is now retired from the US Marine Corps after serving honorably for over 20 years.

Main Dishes

Suzanne Simmons
www.SuzanneSimmons.com
www.ElizabethGuest.net

Suzanne's Famous Sloppy Joe's

Ingredients:

2 lbs. of ground beef (In attempt to make these sandwiches as healthy as possible, I use the leanest ground beef I can find. Usually 96% fat free.)
1 can of tomato paste (12 oz. size)
1 3/4 cups Ketchup
1/3 cup minced onion (Sometimes I take a short cut and use dried minced onion.)
3 tbsp. of sweet relish
3-4 tbsp. of finely chopped celery
2 tbsp. of brown sugar
3/4 tsp. of garlic powder
1/4 tsp. of chili powder
1/2 of a green bell pepper, diced
One dozen hamburger buns

Optional: 12 slices of the cheese of your choice (I use fat free Cheddar in another bow to health.)

Directions:

Brown the ground beef in a large pot. Drain off the excess liquid/fat. Add all the other ingredients and cook, stirring occasionally, until the mixture is bubbly hot. Spoon mixture onto hamburger buns, adding a slice of cheese if desired, and serve.

Makes at least 12 sandwiches.

Elizabeth Elias, Reader

Santa Fe Chili

Ingredients:

2 lbs. chicken cut up in 1/2 in. cubes
4 red peppers
4 green peppers
1 oz. garlic salt
2 large chopped onions
3 tbsp. chili powder
3 tsp. cumin
1/4 tsp. cayenne pepper
1 can diced tomatoes, undrained
2 (14 1/2 oz.) cans chicken broth
2 cans kidney beans washed and drained
1 (12oz.) jar salsa
1 (10oz.) pkg. corn
1/2 tsp. salt
1/2 tsp. pepper.

Directions:

Sauté chicken in 1/2 cup oil. Add chopped onion. Add all other ingredients.

Cook over med-low heat for approx 1 hour.

Makes 16 servings. Recipe can be cut in half.

Jules Bennett
www.julesbennett.com

Chicken and Rice

Ingredients:

1/2 stick margarine
4-6 chicken breasts
1 cup rice, uncooked
1 pkg. Onion Soup mix
Cream of Celery, Mushroom or Chicken Soup

Directions:

Melt margarine in 9x13 pan.
Add rice (uncooked).
Place chicken in pan over rice.
Dilute soup with enough water to make 2 cups of liquid.
Pour over chicken.
Top with onion soup mix (dry).

Bake at 400 degrees for 1 hour.

Author Note:

May require adding a little more water to rice about halfway through baking.

Sue-Ellen Welfonder
www.welfonder.com

Steak and Ale Pie
(just like in a cozy Highland pub)

Prep time: 30 min to 1 hour

Cooking time: over 2 hours

Ingredients:

2 lbs. good stewing steak (room temperature)
Vegetable oil
1 medium onion, peeled and diced
1 tbsp. all-purpose flour
1 tbsp. ketchup
1 tbsp. Worcestershire sauce
Fresh thyme, marjoram and chopped parsley to your own
    taste
1 tsp. brown (or any strong-flavored) mustard
1 bay leaf
Salt and cracked black peppercorns (just a dash of each)
1/4 pint beef stock
1/4 pint ale
1/2 lb. sliced mushrooms
1 lb. puff pastry (readymade works fine)

Directions:

Step One: Cut the steak into 1 in. cubes, then heat the oil in a saucepan and fry the onion until just glassy. Now add the beef, making sure the meat and cook until medium brown. Add the flour and stir until dark brown (about 1 minute).

Now add in the ketchup, Worcestershire sauce, thyme, marjoram, mustard, bay leaf and seasoning. Slowly add the beef stock and ale and bring to boil.

Next come the mushrooms. Now simmer gently until the beef is almost tender, approx. 1 1/2 hours.

Step Two: Preheat oven to 400 degrees F (200 C) then remove the meat from the heat, skimming off any excess fat. Adjust seasonings to taste and add the fresh chopped parsley. Pour the meat mixture into a low casserole/pie dish and cover with the pastry, carefully trimming the edges.

Bake for 20-25 minutes or until pastry is 'puffed' and golden brown.

Enjoy with a pint of real ale and candlelight.

Allie Mackay
www.alliemackay.com

Stovies
(an easy Scottish dish for leftovers—this can
be prepared the night before)

Ingredients:

Leftover meat (roast beef is best)
1-2 onions, sliced
Leftover mashed potatoes
2 "Oxo" beef cubes
Skim milk
Unsalted butter

Directions:

Using the leftover meat, make stovies for the following night. Caramelize sliced onions and add them with the chopped remains of the leftover beef to mashed potatoes that have had a couple of **"Oxo" beef cubes crumbled into the mixture. Add skim milk to taste and plenty of **unsalted butter.

**Any beef cubes will do, "Oxo" is the British brand I use. The beef cubes give the mix an intense flavoring and so salt is not needed.

Julie Leto
www.julieleto.com &
www.marisela.info

Mediterranean Chicken Wraps

This is an easy recipe that you can make for a quick lunch for yourself and friends (delicious to serve with Greek Lemon Soup and a Greek Salad) or to roll and cut into bite size pieces for a party. I don't have amounts listed because I just put on as much as I personally like! I serve the wraps with small bowl of balsamic vinegar, which gives a great sweet acidic contrast to the creamy cheeses.

Ingredients:

Tomato-Basil Tortillas
Soft Cream Cheese
Pesto (fresh or bottled)
Goat Cheese
Roasted Chicken Breast (either from the deli or a store-bought rotisserie chicken)
Sun Dried Tomatoes (jarred with olive oil)
Balsamic Vinegar

Directions:

Take a tomato-basic wrap and spread a layer of cream cheese, keeping about an inch from the sides. Spread pesto to taste, then crumble on goat cheese. Add in shredded chicken from the rotisserie (or sliced chicken from deli) and then layer on a confetti of sun dried tomatoes, sliced into ribbons. Roll the wrap, then put in the fridge to let it set if you're going to slice smaller to serve at a party. If you're going to have it for lunch, roll and enjoy! Dip in balsamic vinegar for an extra splash of flavor. Enjoy!

Rosey Haggerty

Hot Crabmeat Puffs

Ingredients:

1 regular can (tuna sized) or pkg. of crabmeat
1 stick of softened butter
2 garlic cloves, chopped fine (more cloves if you love garlic) or a quarter tsp of garlic powder
1 tbsp. mayonnaise
1 small jar of Olde English Chedder (made by Kraft and usually in the 'cool' section with cheeses, etc.)
1 pkg. of English muffins

Directions:

Mix together all wet ingredients.

Spread on the muffin halves, cut them into quarters, put them on a baking sheet, cover with foil, and put in freezer.

Whenever you want them, put frozen puffs into a preheated 350 or 375 degree oven, for about 20 minutes, or until slightly browned.

Joanne Rock
www.joannerock.com

Parmesan Polenta

4 servings

Ingredients:

1 1/3 cups yellow corn meal
1 tbsp. granulated sugar
1/2 tsp. salt, or to taste (optional)
3 cups water
1 cup 1% fat milk
1 medium onion, diced
1/4 cup (1 oz.) grated Parmesan cheese

Directions:

In a 3-qt. microwave-safe casserole, combine corn meal, sugar, salt, if desired, water, milk, and onion. Stir to mix well.

Cook, uncovered, on full power for 8 to 9 minutes; stop and stir with a wire whisk after 3 minutes and 6 minutes. Stir again with a wire whisk until mixture is smooth. Whisk in cheese. Cover with casserole top, and cook an additional 4 to 5 minutes on high power. Remove from microwave, and let stand an additional 2 or 3 minutes.

Ann M. Warner
www.annwarner.com

Sweet Potato Casserole

This makes a yummy addition to a Thanksgiving feast or to any meal. The recipe comes, as do so many things from a friend of a friend.

Ingredients & Directions:

3 cups cooked sweet potatoes (no skin) (Cube and cook in boiling water until soft)
1/2 cup sugar
1/2 tsp. salt
1/2 stick butter softened (low-fat butter may be used)
1/2 cup milk
2 eggs

Mash the hot sweet potatoes with the rest of the ingredients (like mashed potatoes).

Topping:

1 cup chopped pecans
1/3 cup flour
1/2 cup brown sugar
1/2 stick softened butter

Use pastry blender or spatula to blend above ingredients together.

Put sweet potato mix in lightly greased casserole dish. Top with topping. Bake at 350 degrees for 35 minutes.

Brenda Williamson
www.BrendaWilliamson.com

Hash-Brown Casserole Breakfast

Ingredients:

2 lb. frozen shredded hash-browns
1/2 cup margarine, melted
1 tsp. salt
1/2 tsp. black pepper
1/4 cup finely chopped onion
1 can cream of chicken soup
8 oz. of bulk sausage, cooked until crumbly
8 oz. cheddar cheese, grated (or your favorite cheese)

Directions:

Spray 9x13 baking pan with nonstick cooking spray.
Combine soup, margarine, salt, pepper, onion and cheese.
Gently mix in the potatoes and pour into prepared pan.
Bake in 350 degrees in a preheated oven for 45 minutes.

Author Note:

Perfect for breakfast for large groups.

Ann M. Warner
www.annwarner.com

Forgotten Chicken

This is a great, cook-all-afternoon meal. It comes from a friend of my mother's.

Several chicken pieces, legs or thighs are best, skin removed.
1 1/2 cup brown rice (white rice may be substituted)
chopped onion, celery, and carrot
2 cup cream soup (Cream of mushroom works well)
1 1/2 cup water
1 pkg. onion soup mix

Wash rice, place in the bottom of a roasting pan with the onion, celery, and carrots. Mix soups and water and add to the pan. Place chicken on top of the soup/rice mix. Sprinkle paprika on top.

Cindy Carver
www.ManifestingGoals.com

Mac & Cheese Casserole

Cover and bake at 350 degrees for 2 hrs without looking.

1 - box of Mac & Cheese
1 - can of cream of mushroom or celery soup
1 - can of tuna

Make the box of Mac & Cheese as directed.
Mix all ingredients.
Heat and eat.

Ann M. Warner
www.annwarner.com

Hot Chicken Salad

Ingredients:

1 cup diced celery
3/4 cup mayonnaise (Hellman's Light works well)
1 can cream of mushroom soup
1 tbsp. chopped onion
2 tsp. lemon juice
1 can water chestnuts, chopped
Grated cheese to taste, cheddar or Jack work well
1 cup cubed, cooked chicken

Directions:

Mix all the ingredients and place in a greased pan or baking dish. Top with sliced almonds, or leave plain. Bake at 350 degrees for 35 min.

Author Note:

Here's a good way to use up leftover cooked chicken. The result is slightly crunchy, and doesn't seem like eating leftovers at all.

Ann M. Warner
www.annwarner.com

Salmon (or Tuna) Casserole

Ingredients:

12 oz. can of salmon or tuna drained
1 cup chopped celery
1 cup chopped fresh or canned pears (diced apple may be substituted)
1/2 cup pecan halves or walnuts (may be left out)
1/4 cup chopped onion
1 cup shredded cheddar or cubed Velveeta cheese
3/4 cup mayonnaise (Hellman's Light Mayonnaise works well
2 tbsp. lemon juice

Directions:

Mix all ingredients and bake for 20 min at 425 degrees. The casserole will be bubbly, cheesy, and slightly runny.

Author Note:

I got this recipe from a gourmet dinner club, and have been making it ever since, during Lent as well as the rest of the year. The surprise ingredient is the pears which have a magical effect on the flavor.

Becky Barker
www.beckybarker.com

Spaghetti Pizza

Ingredients:

1/4 to 1/2 lb. of spaghetti, cooked and drained
1 can or jar of ready-made pizza sauce
12 oz. of mozzarella or provolone cheese
Parmesan Cheese to taste
Pepperoni, mushrooms or any favorite pizza topping.

Directions:

Spray a 9X13 pan (small cookie sheet or pizza pan) with non-stick spray and spread the spaghetti noodles, then pat them down to make a crust. You can make a thin layer or a thick layer. Sometimes I also toss the spaghetti with a little parmesan before layering it. Then spread the sauce, cheese and toppings over the spaghetti. Finish with a light dusting of parmesan cheese. Bake at 375 degrees for 15-20 minutes until the cheese is browned.

This is also a great recipe for leftover spaghetti and meat sauce. I combine the noodles and sauce to make my crust and then add cheese and toppings to taste.

Author Note:

This has always been a huge favorite for my family. It's really simple, feeds a crowd (sports teams!) and is relatively inexpensive to make.

Heather Grothaus
www.HeatherGrothaus.com

Venison Summer Sausage

As any wife whose husband deer hunts will attest, you get a lot of ground meat from a single deer. A dilemma if, like me, you can't stand the stuff! This is the only recipe using ground venison that I actually like—it tastes way better than the store bought stuff, and you know what's in it! Awesome as an appetizer or snack with cheese and crackers. You can also slice it thin for sandwiches.

Ingredients:

2 lbs. ground venison
1 cup cold water
2 tbsp. Morton's TenderQuick salt
1 tsp. garlic salt
1 tsp. pepper
1 tsp. onion salt
2 tsp. Liquid Smoke
Crushed red pepper or cayenne to taste

Directions:

Combine all ingredients and mix well. Place in a covered dish and let stand in the refrigerator for 24-48 hours (48 hours is best). Divide mixture equally into three parts. Shape into rolls with aluminum foil (so that they resemble rolls of breakfast-type sausage). Twist the ends up tight. Poke holes along the bottom of each roll with a fork to allow grease to drain (there won't be much). Place rolls on a broiler pan and bake at 325 degrees for 1 1/2 hours. Store in plastic bags in fridge. Can also be frozen.

Heather Grothaus
www.HeatherGrothaus.com

Cincinnati Chili

Ingredients:

1 lb. ground beef
1 medium onion, chopped
1/4 tsp. garlic powder
8 oz. tomato sauce
2-4 cup water
1 tbsp. chili powder
1/2 tbsp. paprika
1 tsp. pepper
1/2 tsp. sugar
1/2 tsp. cumin
1/4 tsp. cinnamon
1/2 small bay leaf
1 tbsp. cocoa

Directions:

Sprinkle some salt in the bottom of a large pot and add beef, onion, and garlic powder. Brown, drain, and blend in processor or blender (in batches—it's messy) for a few seconds. Return to pot and add 1 cup of water and remaining ingredients. Simmer at least 2 hours, uncovered, adding remaining water, 1 cup at a time, as it simmers down. Remove bay leaf before serving—over spaghetti or hot dogs, of course! Top with lots of finely shredded cheddar.

C. J. Winters
www.cjwinters.com

Shrimpburgers

Ingredients:

12 oz. frozen cooked shrimp (I use up to 16 oz.)
3 tbsp. butter or margarine
3 tbsp. flour
3/4 cup milk
1 cup cooked rice
1/2 cup grated processed cheese
2 tbsp. grated onion
1/2 tsp. salt
1/8 tsp. pepper (I use more as the flavor is quite bland)
Dash cayenne powder (I use a heavy dash)
Dry breadcrumbs

Directions:

Cut shrimp into small pieces. Melt butter, stir in flour, add milk gradually. Cook until thick, stirring, then cool and combine with remaining ingredients.
Chill for easier handling.
Shape into 6 flat patties and coat with breadcrumbs. Fry in hot oil, browning on both sides. Serve in toasted hamburger buns.

NOTE: These are very soft 'burgers and tend to fall apart.

Catherine Mann
www.CatherineMann.com

Chicken Curry Casserole

Ingredients:

2 pkgs. (10 oz. each) frozen broccoli, cooked, patted dry
6 boneless chicken breasts, boiled & cubed
1 can cream of chicken soup
1 can cream of celery soup
1 cup Miracle Whip
1 tsp. lemon juice
1 tsp. curry powder

TOPPING:

1 cup bread crumbs
2 tbsp. butter or margarine
6 oz. grated cheese

Directions:

Preheat over to 350 degrees. Place cooked broccoli on bottom of a 13X9 pan. Place cubed chicken on top. Mix soups, juice, powder and Miracle Whip. Pour over top. Sprinkle bread crumbs and cheese of tops. Dot with butter/margarine. Cook at 350 degrees for 30 minutes. Can prepare the casserole earlier in the day, cover with tin foil and store in the refrigerator until ready to bake. Simply bake an extra 10 minutes.

Monica Flowers, Lori Foster's sister
"Our mother altered this once while visiting, and I've used her altered recipe ever since."

Cheesy Chicken Bake with Vegetables

Ingredients:

10 chicken tenders or 4 boneless, skinless chicken breasts
10.5 oz. can of cream of mushroom or cream of chicken soup
16 oz. bag of frozen peas or any frozen vegetable or combination you prefer
8 oz. sour cream
8 oz. (approx. 2 cups) shredded cheddar, sharp or mild
1 1/2 cup all purpose baking mix (Jiffy, Bisquick, or any generic store brand will do)
Milk

Directions:

Preheat oven to 450 degrees.
Boil chicken until tender. Add frozen vegetables approx. last 8 minutes of cooking.
In a large, deep, cast iron skillet, add soup, sour cream, and about 1/2 cup of milk. Add more milk if necessary to make a soupy mix.
Drain chicken and peas when done, and add to mixture in skillet.
Sprinkle shredded cheese evenly over top of that.
In a separate bowl, add just enough milk to the baking mix to make it thick but pourable.
Drizzle over cheese and put into oven.
Bake until top is crusty and browned.

Jill Shalvis
www.jillshalvis.com

Yummy Breakfast Casserole

Ingredients & Directions:

1 layer of tater tots
1 layer of ham or sausage cubes
1 layer of grated cheddar cheese

Pour this over the layers:

6 beaten eggs
1/2 tsp. salt
1/2 tsp. pepper
1 tsp. dry mustard
1/2 cup chopped onion
3 cups of milk
2 tsp. Worcestershire sauce

Add 1/2 cup melted butter over all that. Cook 1 hour at 350 degrees uncovered

Jaci Burton
www.jaciburton.com

Spaghetti with Meat Sauce

Ingredients:

1-2 lbs. Hamburger (depends on how thick you want your
   meat sauce)
1 16 oz. can tomato sauce
1 16 oz. can tomato paste
1 stick margarine or butter
4 tbsp. Extra Virgin Olive Oil
1 clove garlic, chopped fine
1/4 onion
1 tsp. salt
1 tsp. pepper
1 tbsp. Italian Seasoning
1 lb. spaghetti noodles
Fresh parmesan cheese

Directions:

Brown hamburger and pour off fat. Set it aside.
In a large sauce pan, Melt butter
Add Olive oil
Sauté garlic and onions in butter and oil until lightly
browned
Add tomato sauce and tomato paste
Add salt, pepper and Italian Seasoning
Add 1 can of water, bring to a boil, then simmer for 30
minutes.
After sauce has simmered, add hamburger to sauce and
continue to simmer.
Cook noodles according to package directions. (You can do
this while you're simmering sauce)
Pour meat sauce over cooked noodles. Sprinkle parmesan
cheese over top and serve.
Side dishes – Fresh garden salad and Italian bread or
French bread
Bon Appetite!

Karen Harper
www.karenharperauthor.com

Pasta Putanesca

Ingredients:

1/4 cup olive oil
1 clove garlic, crushed
1/4 cup (or less) chopped red onion
1 tbsp. red wine vinegar
2 tbsp. (or less) sugar
1 1/2 cups (or more) chopped tomatoes (or canned, not
   drained)
1/4 cup sliced black olives
Parsley, fresh or dried
Oregano & basil to taste
1 can of drained tuna, shrimp or other seafood

Directions:

Simmer garlic in olive oil, add other ingredients and let
simmer for 5-10 minutes. Prepare pasta (I use fettuccini). Pour
sauce over pasta. Makes 2 large servings.

Karin Tabke
www.karintabke.com

Karin's mom's fabo Maryland crab cakes!

Ingredients:

8 oz. of crabmeat. This recipe is best if you use Maryland blue crab meat, or the jumbo lump.
Strain crab meat and set aside.

In a large bowl mix:
1 egg
2 tsp. Worcestershire sauce
1/2 tsp. dry mustard
2 tbsp. mayo, set a tad aside (don't use the salad dressing *bleck*, or the fat free stuff *double bleck*, use Kraft)
1 tsp. lemon juice
2 tsp. yellow mustard
3 tsp. melted butter (don't use margarine, use the real stuff)
1 tsp. parsley
1 tsp. Old Bay, I usually sprinkle in 2

Directions:

With a wire whisk mix thoroughly, then add the crab and mix again (use your hands and dig in) then add 1/3 cup regular bread crumbs. Form into crab cakes. Brush the tops with a swipe of the mayo and then sprinkle a light dusting of paprika on cakes (makes them purdy). Some people like to pan fry, I like mine baked. Heat oven to 350 degrees, put cakes on a cookie sheet and bake for 12-15 min.

Then enjoy!

(Oh, and these are great heated up the next day on fresh white bread with a smattering of tartar sauce.)

Mary Campisi
www.marycampisi.com

Penne Pasta with Spinach

Ingredients:

4 Cloves finely chopped Garlic
1 medium Onion finely chopped
3-4 tbsp. Olive Oil
4 large Tomatoes (Chopped) or 1 1/2 large cans diced tomatoes (32 oz. Cans)
1 can Garbanzo beans (Cici beans), drained and rinsed
1 lb. of fresh spinach with stems removed and steamed (may sub frozen cooked spinach)
1 lb. Penne pasta
Romano Cheese
Salt & Pepper

Directions:

Sauté onion in olive oil over low/medium heat until clear. Add garlic and simmer 1-2 minutes. Add tomatoes and cook until softened. Salt and Pepper to taste. Add garbanzo beans. Add cooked spinach to hot mixture. Add cooked pasta, mix well. Serve with Romano cheese.

Susanne Marie Knight
http://www.susanneknight.com

Chicken Pad Thai to the Max!

Ingredients:

1 tbsp. peanut butter, creamy
1 tbsp. soy sauce
1 tsp. Asian chili paste
1 tbsp. water
3 tbsp. peanut or cooking oil
1 tsp. garlic powder
1 tsp. ginger powder
1 cup carrots
1 boneless, skinless chicken breast, cut into thin strips
3/4 lb. linguine, cooked
1 tbsp. brown sugar
1 tbsp. cider vinegar
2 cups bean sprouts
Chopped peanuts for topping

Directions:

Mix peanut butter, soy sauce, chili paste and water together until smooth. Set aside.
Heat pan or wok over medium heat, then add oil.
Once hot, stir in ginger and garlic and cook for one minute.
Add carrots and chicken to stir-fry for about three minutes.
Add noodles. Stir, and continue to cook.
Add peanut/chili sauce, brown sugar and cider vinegar. Stir to coat.
Serve with bean spouts and top with chopped peanuts.

Note: In my paranormal romantic suspense COMPETITORS!, both Vivianne and Max enjoy Chicken Pad Thai. Try this different version of this classic dish from Thailand and see if you don't fall in love with it, too!

Susanne Marie Knight
http://www.susanneknight.com

Timeless Brunch or Ham and Egg Casserole

Ingredients:

10 slices white bread, decrusted and cut into cubes
3 cup cubed ham
3 cup milk
1 cup Velvida Cheese
1/2 cup onion, chopped
3/4 tsp. dry mustard
1 cup cheddar cheese, shredded
Pinch pepper
1/2 tsp. salt

Directions:

Preheat oven to 325 degrees.
Mix ingredients together, then pour into greased 9x13 in. pan.
Refrigerate.
Bake for one hour until firm.

Note: In my 5 star, PEARL award nominee time-travel Regency TIMELESS DECEPTION, Alaina often breakfasted on ham and eggs. Here is a delicious recipe that includes just about everything you need for a hearty morning meal.

Susanne Marie Knight
www.susanneknight.com

Fowl Indigestion or Roast Cornish Hens

Ingredients:

2 Rock Cornish Game hens
2 tbsp. butter, melted
1 pkg. (6 oz.) wild rice mix
1/4 cup honey
2 tbsp. orange juice
1/4 cup barbecue sauce
1 tsp. salt

Directions:

Prepare rice as directed.
Rinse birds and pat dry.
Sprinkle cavity with 1/2 tsp. salt and stuff loosely 3/4 full with rice.
Tie legs together and place in roasting pan.
Brush with butter and roast at 400 degrees for 30 minutes.
Combine honey, juice, and sauce.
Baste every 5 minutes for 15 to 20 more minutes.
When done, place birds on platter, untie legs and surround with remaining rice.

Note: In my five-star time-travel Regency LORD DARVER'S MATCH, Hillary fears her strange predicament is really just a nightmare: indigestion caused by a Cornish hen dinner. Not to worry; this delicious recipe is too tasty to give you anything but a full belly!

Cheyenne McCray
cheyennemccray.com

Sour Cream Chicken Enchiladas

Sauce Ingredients:

2 cans cream of chicken soup
1/2 cup sour cream
1 or 2 cans diced peeled green chilis
1/2 tsp. salt

Combine and heat until sauce is smooth.

Enchilada Ingredients:

1 dozen corn tortillas
2 cups grated cheese
1 can white meat chicken
1 cup chopped olives (optional)
1/2 cup chopped onions (optional)

Directions:

Dip corn tortillas into hot oil. (Dab off excess oil with a paper towel) Put cheese, onions, olives, and chicken in a tortilla and roll. Place in a 13" x 9" pan. Continue until all tortillas have been filled. Pour sauce over the top. Bake 325 degrees for 25 minutes. Makes great re-heated leftovers. Even better the second time!

Tonya Ramagos
http://www.tonyaramagos.com

Balsamic Chicken

Serves 6

Ingredients:

6 boneless, skinless chicken breast halves
1 1/2 tsp. fresh rosemary leaves, minced, or 1/2 tsp. dried
2 cloves garlic, minced
1/2 tsp. freshly ground black pepper
1/2 tsp. salt
2 tbsp. extra-virgin olive oil
4-6 tbsp. white wine (optional)
1/4 cup balsamic vinegar

Directions:

Rinse the chicken and pat dry. Combine the rosemary, garlic, pepper, and salt in a small bowl and mix well. Place the chicken in a large bowl. Drizzle with the oil, and rub with the spice mixture. Cover and refrigerate overnight.

Preheat the oven to 450 degrees. Spray a heavy roasting pan or iron skillet with cooking spray. Place the chicken in the pan and bake for 10 minutes. Turn the chicken over. If the drippings begin to stick to the pan, stir in 3-4 tablespoons water or white wine (if using).

Bake about 10 minutes or until a thermometer inserted in the thickest portion registers 160 degrees and the juices run clear. If the pan is dry, stir in another 1-2 tablespoons of water or white wine to loosen the drippings. Drizzle the vinegar over the chicken in the pan.

Transfer the chicken to plates. Stir the liquid in the pan and drizzle over the chicken.

Janice Maynard
www.janicemaynard.com

Lasagna For Picky Eaters

Ingredients & Directions:

Brown one pound of ground beef and drain well. Salt with a bit of garlic salt, regular salt, and pepper. Add one can of tomato paste and one can of tomato sauce and two paste cans of water. Mix well. Cook 6 ounces of Ronco wide egg noodles (or equivalent) according to directions—drain. In baking dish (I use my 9 1/2 inch square white Pyrex one) put half of the meat sauce, all of the noodles spread evenly, 12 ounces of cottage cheese spread in a thin layer, and one 8 ounce package of sliced Swiss cheese placed over all... add the rest of the meat sauce. Cover the top with a generous covering of parmesan cheese. I put enough that I can no longer see the meat sauce.

Bake uncovered one hour at 350 degrees. Sometimes this will bubble over a tiny bit, so you might want to put the dish on a layer of foil to protect your oven. This lasagna is especially good the second day as leftovers... if there is any left!

Toni Leland
www.tonileland.com

Deadline Crockpot Chicken

Serves 6
Prep Time: 5 hrs

Ingredients:

4 lbs. whole fryer chicken
2 tbsp. Grill Mate Citrus Garlic Seasoning (or other flavor)

Directions:

Rinse the chicken and set into the crockpot tail first; adjust chicken so that breast is not touching the sides of the pot.

Sprinkle the seasoning over and cover. Do not add liquid.

Cook on high for 1 hour, then turn to low and cook for 3-4 more hours.
Turn off heat and allow to cool for awhile.

Using large spoons or spatulas, turn the chicken over so the breast meat is in the juice. This prevents the white meat from drying out and the juice soaks into the meat.

Author Note:

Melts in your mouth. Wonderful served at room temperature, or reheated.

Cathy Liggett
www.cathyliggett.com

Not the Same Old Mac & Cheese

Ingredients:

12 oz. wide egg noodles
2 cups heavy cream
2 1/2 cups whole milk
2 tsp. all-purpose flour
1/2 tsp. salt
1/4 tsp. ground black pepper
2 cups (packed) grated Fontina*
3/4 cup (packed) finely grated Parmesan
3/4 cup (packed) grated mozzarella
4 oz. cooked ham, diced, optional
2 tbsp. finely chopped fresh parsley leaves

*if can't find, substitute another "white" cheese, like Monterey Jack

Directions:

Preheat the oven to 450 degrees.
Butter a 13 by 9-inch glass baking. Cook the noodles in a large pot of boiling salted water until tender but still firm to bite, stirring frequently, about 5 minutes.
Drain well, but do not rinse.

Whisk the cream, milk, flour, 1/2 tsp. salt, and pepper in large bowl to blend. Stir in 1 cup Fontina, 1/2 cup Parmesan, 1/2 cup mozzarella, ham, if using, and parsley. Add the noodles and toss to coat. Transfer the noodle mixture to the prepared baking dish. Toss the remaining 1 cup Fontina, 1/4 cup Parmesan, and 1/4 cup mozzarella in a small bowl to blend. Sprinkle the cheese mixture over the noodle mixture. Bake until the sauce bubbles and the cheese melts and begins to brown on top, about 20 minutes. Let stand for 10 minutes before serving.

Susan Elizabeth Phillips
www.susanephillips.com

COLIN BYRNE'S Spicy Pasta (Vegetarian)

Ingredients:

About 3/4 of a bag of whole wheat rotini** (Both Colin and
I prefer Bella Terra Organic.)
2 (14 oz.) cans STEWED tomatoes with Italian seasoning, if
available. (Don't used diced tomatoes.)
Lots of fresh garlic sliced. (Original recipe calls for 2 cloves.
I use about 6)
Red pepper flakes to taste (1/2 tsp. Colin and Sugar Beth
love it spicy.)
1/2 cup sliced pitted olives and/or capers to taste
2 tbsp. olive oil

Directions:

1. Boil water for pasta
2. In large skillet or medium saucepan, sauté red pepper
flakes and sliced fresh garlic in olive oil until golden. Don't burn
it. (HINT: To get garlic smell out of your fingers, rub your fingers
against sides of stainless steel sink. No, I'm not kidding, and
don't ask me why.)
3. Add stewed tomatoes. Bring to boil, then turn down heat
and simmer for 15-20 minutes while pasta is cooking. Break up
tomatoes when spoon.
4. When sauce has slightly thickened, it's ready to serve.
Spoon pasta into bowls. Toss olives or capers over hot pasta,
then ladle on sauce. (Bill loves the olives, but I prefer capers
because of their zing and low fat content.)
5. If desired, top with a little parmesan or feta

**I'm only cooking with rotini these days. I got tired of
trying to keep spaghetti from dangling down my chin or
splashing on my clothes. Even when I go out to eat, I'll ask the
kitchen to substitute rotini. It's so much easier to handle.

Author Note:

This is not only one of Colin's favorite dishes, but my husband Bill's as well. Because it's quick and easy, Colin frequently fixes this on nights when it's his turn to cook. (Husband Bill, unfortunately, is cooking challenged.) Sugar Beth even loves this entree, despite the fact that it's incredibly healthy. Colin, being a guy, doesn't measure.... Serves 2 people with huge appetites or 3 people who eat normally.

Cindi Myers
www.CindiMyers.com

Buttermilk Baked Chicken

Ingredients:

Chicken parts
1 can cream of chicken soup
1 pint buttermilk
2 tbsp. flour
1/2 tsp. Season Salt
2 tbsp. butter

Directions:

Combine the flour and Season Salt. Dip chicken parts in buttermilk, then in seasoned flour. Melt butter in skillet. Brown chicken in butter. When chicken is browned, place in baking dish and bake at 350 degrees, uncovered, for 30 minutes. Combine 1 can cream of chicken soup and 1 can buttermilk. Pour over chicken and bake an additional 30 minutes. Serve over rice or mashed potatoes.

Susan Elizabeth Phillips
www.susanephillips.com

WIND LAKE BED & BREAKFAST Baked Oatmeal
(Courtesy of Molly Somerville Tucker)

Ingredients:

6 cups old-fashioned rolled oats
2 cups skimmed milk
2 eggs or 1 cup non-fat egg substitute
3/4 cup brown sugar
1/2 cup unsweetened applesauce
1/4 cup canola oil
4 tsp. baking powder
1 tsp. salt
1 tsp. vanilla
Ground cinnamon
(Optional: raisins, prunes, chopped apples, pecans)

Directions:

Heat oven to 350 degrees. Combine all ingredients except cinnamon in large mixing bowl. Mix well. Place in 13 X 9 inch pan coated with non-stick spray and spread evenly. Sprinkle with cinnamon. Bake until knife inserted in center comes out clean, 30-35 minutes. Serve with milk. Can be made the night before and reheated or frozen.

Note: Michigan mornings can be chilly, even in the summer, and we thank Molly for sharing this recipe to warm up her guests before they take a plunge in the lake. For busy mornings, this can be made day before and refrigerated. Microwave individual portions when ready to serve.

Susan Elizabeth Phillips
www.susanephillips.com

MAT JORIK'S BACHELOR DAYS
Rice In a Skillet
(Version 1)

LUCY'S VERSION:
2 cans (4 cups) Chicken or vegetable broth
1 medium onion diced
2 -3 tbsp. olive oil
2 red pepper diced (optional)
1-2 cups frozen green beans (precook a little in microwave first)
1 cup frozen peas
2 cups rice (I use pearl rice I buy in bags in Mexican food section)
1 tbsp. basil
1/2 tbsp. oregano
garlic, salt, pepper to taste
Optional toppings: a bit of grated cheese and or diced fresh tomatoes

Directions:

Heat oven to 500 degrees. Heat broth in separate pan. In 10-12 inch iron skillet, sauté onion, red pepper, and spices in olive oil. When onion is transparent, add rice, stirring occasionally, for about 1 minute. Add other vegetables and warm broth. Stir and transfer to oven. Bake until all liquid is absorbed and rice is dry on top. About 25 minutes. Optional toppings could include a bit of grated cheese and/or diced fresh tomatoes

Note: What kind of cook do you think FIRST LADY's Mat Jorik might have been before Nealy's staff relieved him of the burden? Since Mat's a no-nonsense guy, I think this might have appealed to him. I love this recipe because it's prepared and baked in the same pan-a big old iron skillet. I think Lucy would prefer Version One while Baby Butt would love gumming on Version Two.

Susan Elizabeth Phillips
www.susanephillips.com

MAT JORIK'S BACHELOR DAYS
Rice in a Skillet
(Version 2)

BUTTON'S VERSION
(Same principle, completely different taste)
3 cups (1 1/2 cans) chicken or vegetable broth
2-3 tbsp. olive oil
1 medium onion diced
1 diced small to medium sweet potato
1 cup rice (I like bagged pearl rice from Mexican food section)
1 cup green beans or peas (If using frozen green beans, pre cook in micro a few minutes)
1 tbsp. basil
1/2 tbsp. oregano
About 2 tbsp. balsamic vinegar
About 1 tbsp. Worcestershire sauce
Salt, pepper to taste

Directions:

Heat oven to 500 degrees. Heat broth in separate pan. In 10-12 inch iron skillet, sauté onion, and spices in olive oil. When onion is transparent, add rice, stirring occasionally, for about 1 minute. Add sweet potato, vegetables warm broth, Balsamic vinegar and Worcestershire. Stir and transfer to oven. Bake until all liquid is absorbed and rice is dry on top. About 25 minutes.

Note: What kind of cook do you think FIRST LADY's Mat Jorik might have been before Nealy's staff relieved him of the burden? Since Mat's a no-nonsense guy, I think this might have appealed to him. I love this recipe because it's prepared and baked in the same pan-a big old iron skillet. I think Lucy would prefer Version One while Baby Butt would love gumming on Version Two.

Susan Elizabeth Phillips
www.susanephillips.com

SHELBY TRAVELER'S Light Summertime Pasta

Ingredients & Directions:

COMBINE IN SERVING BOWL:
About 5-6 cups chopped ripe tomatoes
About 1 cup finely chopped sweet onion (I use less)
1/2 cup chopped fresh basil (I use more) or 2 tbsp. dry basil
1/3 cup balsamic vinegar (Or use half Balsamic and half Rice Vinegar. Don't use cider vinegar. It's too strong.)
1/4 cup oil (I used half olive oil and half canola-both good heart healthy oils)
1-2 tsp. granulated sugar
About 3 minced garlic cloves (to taste)
Salt & freshly ground pepper

Let these ingredients sit on counter at room temperature for about an hour.

Cook about 3/4 pound of a thinner pasta such as angel hair, thin spaghetti, or a smaller rotini in salted water. Drain but don't rinse. Gently toss in serving bowl with above ingredients. Dish onto individual plates and top with grated Parmesan or mozzarella.

Note: As some of you may remember, Shelby Traveler, in LADY BE GOOD, has had a little trouble taking off the weight that accumulated during her pregnancy. Since Shelby loves good food, but also wants to slim down, I know she'll enjoy this recipe. (Note that this tastes best if you let first series of ingredients sit out at room temperature for about 1 hour before serving)

Susan Elizabeth Phillips
www.susanephillips.com

GRACIE AND JILL'S LAZY DAY
Vegetarian Lasagna
(Reduced fat)

This recipe is simple to assemble, but cooking plus resting time takes at least an hour and a half, so get started early.

Ingredients:

Vegetables of choice. (See below)
1 (48 oz.) jar prepared spaghetti sauce (Prego Extra Chunky)
1 lb. low fat cottage cheese
8 oz. low fat tofu
Uncooked lasagna noodles (How many you use depends on size of pan. You don't need an entire package)
About 2 cups shredded mozzarella
About 1/2 cup grated Parmesan cheese
1 cup water

Directions:

1. Using large skillet, sauté vegetables of choice in Pam. (*I use about 1 lb. mushrooms, 1 green pepper, and a box of thawed chopped spinach drained. Sometimes I use a diced eggplant. Jill adds extra onion.)
2. Add spaghetti sauce to vegetables
3. With potato masher, mash tofu and cottage cheese together in medium bowl. Set aside.
4. Spoon about 1 1/2 cups vegetable mixture in bottom of lasagna pan.
5. Cover with layer of noodles.
6. Top with 1/2 of ricotta/tofu mixture
7. Add 1/3 of vegetable sauce.
8. Layer of noodles
9. Rest of ricotta/tofu mixture
10. 1/2 of mozzarella
11. 1/3 of vegetable sauce

12. Layer of noodles
13. Rest of vegetable sauce.

Pour 1 cup of water around sides of pan. Cover tightly with foil. Bake in preheated 350 degree oven for 1 hour. Uncover. Top with rest of Mozzarella and parmesan. Bake 20 minutes more uncovered until bubbly. Let stand 15-20 minutes. Serve.

Note: This recipe should be attractive to busy cooks since you don't have to precook the lasagna noodles. The last time we checked, Gracie Snow Denton, from *Heaven, Texas*, was doing triple duty as a wife, mother, and the mayor of Telarosa, Texas. My Vegetarian Lazy Day Lasagna is right up her alley. I also made it for that wonderful historical romance author Jill Barnett when she came to visit, and she enjoyed it so much she's been making it for friends. So, let's have Gracie and Jill share this recipe. (I've also made lots of adjustments to reduce fat.)

Susan Elizabeth Phillips
www.susanephillips.com

BOBBY TOM DENTON'S
Black Bean and Sweet Potato Burritos

Ingredients:

2 large or three medium-sized sweet potatoes peeled and cubed
3+ cups chopped onion
3 or more large cloves of garlic, chopped
1 tbsp.+ minced fresh green chili (I used serranos. For less kick, try jalapenos) 4 t ground cumin
4 tsp. ground coriander
3 cans (15 oz. each) black beans (pinto beans also an option)
2/3 cup lightly packed cilantro leaves (I bought some of the mild flat Italian parsley by mistake and used it anyway. Great for people who aren't crazy about cilantro.)
2-3 tbsp. fresh lemon juice
8 large flour tortillas (I buy the fat free ones)
Your favorite salsa.

Directions:

1. Place the diced, peeled sweet potatoes in a medium saucepan, cover with water, bring to a boil. Simmer for 10 minutes. Drain and set aside.
2. While sweet potatoes are cooking, sauté onions, garlic, chili in a skillet generously sprayed with Pam. Cook until tender, about 7 minutes. Add cumin and coriander. Cook for another 2-3 minutes, stirring frequently so it doesn't stick.
3. In food processor, combine beans, cilantro, lemon juice. Process. Add sweet potatoes and process again. (Alternative: Mash with potato masher for rougher texture.)

4. Stir in onion mixture, salt to taste, and heat to desired temperature in microwave.

5. Warm tortillas in microwave. Fill each tortilla with about 3/4 cup of mixture and serve with salsa.

This recipe provides a different slant on the more common black bean burritos. I like to serve with a salad or a simple plate of raw vegetables. The richness of the sweet potatoes eliminates the need for cheese, but you can certainly top with some Monterey jack or cheddar if you'd like.

Note: Here's a recipe that suits Bobby Tom Denton, from *Heaven, Texas*, just fine. I adapted it for the former Chicago Stars wide-receiver from *Moosewood Restaurant Low Fat Favorites*. I don't measure things too well, so I hope you can deal with approximations!

Lori Wilde
www.loriwilde.com

Wilde Chicken Marsala

Ingredients:

1/8 tsp. black pepper
1/4 tsp. salt
1/4 cup flour
4 chicken breasts, boned, skinless (5 ounces)
1 tbsp. olive oil
1/2 cup Marsala wine
1/2 cup chicken stock, skim fat from top
1/2 cup fresh lime juice
1/2 cup sliced mushrooms
1 tbsp. fresh parsley, chopped

Directions:

Mix together pepper, salt, and flour. Coat chicken with seasoned flour.

In a heavy-bottomed skillet, heat oil. Place chicken breasts in skillet and brown on both sides. Then remove chicken from skillet and set aside.

To the skillet, add wine and stir until the wine is heated. Add juice, stock, and mushrooms. Stir to toss, reduce heat, and cook for about 10 minutes until the sauce is partially reduced.

Return browned chicken breasts to skillet. Spoon sauce over the chicken. Cover and cook for about 5-10 minutes or until chicken is done.

Serve sauce over chicken. Garnish with chopped parsley.

Yield: 4 servings. Serving Size: 1 chicken breast with 1/3 cup sauce serve over warm buttered pasta noodles.

Note: Each serving provides:
Calories: 277
Total fat: 8 g
Saturated fat: 2 g
Cholesterol: 77 mg
Sodium: 304 mg

Karen Kendall
www.karenkendall.com

Barb's Easy Bacon-Cheese Casserole

Preheat oven to 375 degrees.

Ingredients:

4 eggs
1 1/2 cups milk
1 1/2 cups Bisquick
1 pkg. of bacon (at least 12 slices)
4 oz. shredded cheddar cheese

Directions:

Fry the bacon, then crumble it in the bottom of a greased casserole pan. (You can also substitute cooked, crumbled breakfast sausage.) Sprinkle the cheese over the bacon.

Mix the eggs, milk and Bisquick in a bowl until smooth; pour mixture over the bacon/cheese. Bake for 30-35 minutes.

Author Note:

I got this recipe from my mom, who got it from a book – I forget which one. The recipe can also be doubled if you have a crowd coming!

Colleen Collins
www.colleencollins.net
www.writingprivateinvestigators.com

Ziti with Four Cheeses

Toast in 1 tbsp. unsalted butter: 1/2 cup fresh bread crumbs
Toast the crumbs in melted butter in a small skillet over medium heat until golden. Transfer to a bowl and set aside.

Stir together:
1 lb. dry ziti
1/2 stick unsalted butter

Prepare ziti according to package directions, drain and return to the pot. Stir in the butter until the pasta is well coated.

Prepare cheeses:
1/2 cup Fontina cheese, diced into small pieces (so they'll melt quickly)
1/2 cup Asiago cheese, diced into small pieces (so they'll melt quickly)
1/2 cup fresh mozzarella, diced into small pieces (so they'll melt quickly)
Sprinkle the Fontina, Asiago, and mozzarella over the top of the pasta. Cover and warm over low heat for 1-2 minutes, then stir vigorously to melt the cheeses.

Stir into pasta mixture:
1/2 cup Parmigiano-Reggiano, grated
1/2 cup heavy cream
1/4 tsp. ground nutmeg
Kosher or sea salt to taste
Garnish each serving with prepared bread crumbs.
Note: (any medium-size pasta, such as rigatoni or shells, can be substituted for ziti)
Makes about 10 cups. Total time: 30 minutes (quick and easy to make!)

Patricia Lorenz
www.PatriciaLorenz.com

Chicken Salad

Ingredients & Directions:

Cook 6 six boneless, skinless chicken breasts in microwave
Cut in cubes
Soak in Raspberry Vinaigrette Dressing overnight.
Add seedless grapes, chopped celery, and almonds to taste.
Toss with miracle whip light or mayo.

Note: Patricia Lorenz is an internationally-known inspirational, art-of-living writer and speaker. Patricia is the country's top contributor to the Chicken Soup for the Soul books with stories in over 30 of the Chicken Soup books so far. She's had over 400 articles published in numerous magazines and newspapers; is a contributing writer for sixteen Daily Guideposts books and three dozen anthologies; and is an award-winning newspaper columnist.

Patrice Michelle
http://www.patricemichelle.net

Mexican Lasagna

Ingredients:

1 lb. lean ground beef (uncooked)
1 (16 oz.) can refried beans
2 tsp. oregano dried
3/4 tsp. garlic powder
12 uncooked lasagna noodles
2 1/2 cups water
2 1/2 cups picante sauce
2 cups sour cream (regular, not light)
3/4 cup finely sliced green onion
1 can (2.2 oz.) sliced black olives
1 cup shredded Monterey jack cheese

Directions:

Combine first 5 ingredients. Layer 4 noodles in a 13x9x2** pan. Spread 1/2 of meat mixture over the noodles. Layer another 4 noodles and then the other

1/2 meat mixture. Layer with last 4 noodles. Combine water and picante and pour over above. I use a spatula and lift the mixture and noodles to make sure the picante/water goes all the way to the bottom of the dish. THIS is what will cook your noodles and your meat so make sure all areas are covered top to bottom. Cover tightly with aluminum foil.

Bake at 350 degrees for 1 1/2 hours until noodles are tender. Combine olives, onions and sour cream. Spread over cooked lasagna. Spread cheese over that and cook another 5 minutes to melt the cheese.

**Note: I use a glass 13x9x2 dish so I can lift the dish and see that the liquid has gone all the way to the bottom before I put the foil on.

This is my favorite recipe because ALL of the cooking is done in the oven.

No precooking needed!

Lisa Freeman - Reader
"Sweet and tasty, just like a book by Lucy Monroe."

Pineapple Cheese Casserole

Ingredients:

1 can pineapple tidbits, drained, reserve juice
3 tbsp. flour
3 tbsp. pineapple juice
3 tbsp. sugar (can use Splenda)
1 cup shredded sharp cheddar cheese
1/3 cup melted butter
1/2 cup buttery cracker crumbs (Ritz, Townhouse, etc.)

Directions:

Preheat oven to 350 degrees. Drain pineapple, reserving 3 tablespoons juice. Combine sugar and flour; stir in juice. Add cheese and pineapple tidbits. Mix well. Spoon into greased 1 quart casserole. Combine melted butter with cracker crumbs. Sprinkle over pineapple mixture. Bake 20-30 minutes. Serves 4. Can easily be doubled or tripled.

Larissa Ione
www.LarissaIone.com

Mexican Lasagna

Ingredients:

4 cups shredded sharp cheddar cheese
9 -12 uncooked lasagna noodles
1/2 lb. hamburger
1 can black beans
1 onion, chopped
3 cups salsa
1 cup water
Small can sliced olives
Sour cream (optional)

Directions:

Cook hamburger, drain. Add onion and cook until onions are tender. Stir in sauce, water, beans, and 1 cup of cheese.

Spread 1/4 of sauce in bottom of greased 13 x 9 pan. Layer noodles, sauce mixture, cheese. Repeat, ending with sauce and cheese. Sprinkle with olives.

Cover with foil, bake 30 minutes at 350 degrees. Remove cover and bake another 20 minutes. Serve with sour cream, if desired.

Author Note:

This recipe is excellent when the hamburger is replaced with veggie crumbles, but either way, this is a family favorite, and VERY easy to make, which makes it a wonderful dish for guests!

Christine Feehan
www.christinefeehan.com

Mexican Pizza:

Ingredients:

Hamburger
Taco Seasoning Mix
Refried Beans
Tomato Sauce
Four Tortillas
Grated Cheese (your choice)
Olives
Green Onions
Salsa (optional)
Sour Cream (optional)
Diced Tomatoes
Avocado (optional)

Directions:

Brown and drain meat
Reheat in 1/4 cup water with seasoning mix
Add 8 oz. tomato sauce
Cook for 2 minutes
Add refried beans and warm
Add oil in large frying pan and lightly brown flour tortillas- 2 per pizza

Place even layer of beans and meat on tortilla, cover all but outside 1/2".
Place second tortilla on top of first- put even layer of tomato sauce or salsa of choice on top of tortilla.
Add cheese, green onions, olives, and tomatoes.
Place in microwave and cook on high until cheese is melted (approx 1 1/2 min).
Add avocado and sour cream.

Tori Carrington
www.toricarrington.net
www.sofiemetro.com

Pasticcio (Greek Lasagna)

Beef Mixture:

1 tbsp. olive oil
2 lbs. ground chuck or beef
1 small, finely chopped onion
2 finely chopped cloves garlic (to taste)
6 whole cloves
2 tsp. salt
1/2 tsp. pepper
1 (14.5 oz.) can of diced tomatoes

Noodles:

1 lb. Pasticcio noodles (found at any Greek or Italian store)
1 tbsp. salt
1 cup grated Kefalotiri Cheese (or Parmesan)

Besamel:

1/2 cup butter (one stick)
3/4 cup flour
4 hot cups milk
Salt
Pepper
Dash of nutmeg (optional)
1 cup grated Kefalotiri Cheese (or Parmesan)
4 egg yolks

Directions:

For the beef mixture: Heat the olive oil in a large frying pan and sauté the ground beef and onion and garlic until slightly browned. Add remaining ingredients, cover and cook over a medium heat for approximately twenty minutes.

Noodles: Cook pasticcio in salted boiling water until soft but firm. Drain and return to the pan.

Besamel: Melt the butter in a heavy saucepan; add the flour and cook, stirring constantly for 1 minute. Add the milk all at once, and stir until the sauce is smooth. Add salt, pepper and nutmeg. Remove from heat and stir in the cheese and egg yolks.

Sprinkle a 9"x13" Pyrex pan with grated Kefalotiri or Parmesan and put in half the pasticcio. Sprinkle with Kefalotiri or Parmesan and cover with half the beef mixture. Repeat with the rest of the pasticcio and beef mixture and Kefalotiri. Spoon besamel over the top and sprinkle that with the rest of the cheese and cook at in 350 degree oven for about 45 minutes or until golden brown. Let settle for 20 minutes and then cut into square pieces and serve. Kali Orixi!

Christine Feehan
http://www.christinefeehan.com

Chicken Enchiladas:

Ingredients:

3 Chicken Breasts
30 Corn Tortillas
Large can cream of chicken soup
Green or Red Enchilada Sauce (large can)
Green onions- 3 or 4 cut up
Garlic- 4 cloves crushed and cut up
Parsley-1/2 cup
Cilantro- tbsp. or two
Monterey Jack Cheese- 2 cups
Cheddar Cheese- 2 cups
Parmesan Cheese- 1 cup
Olives- 1 to 2 cans cut up
1/2 cup milk
2 chicken bouillon cubes (dissolved in 1/8 cup water)

Directions:

Boil chicken breasts- cool and de-bone
Cut into 1" squares
In large microwave bowl, add chicken, soup, enchiladas sauce, green onions, parsley, cilantro, bouillon cube mix, milk and garlic
Heat in microwave and stir until warm.
In a large 9x13 baking pan add olive oil or non-stick spray in bottom of pan
Put tortillas in single layer in pan. Break up tortillas in quarters to fill gaps.
Scoop thin layer of mixture over tortillas- separate chicken evenly and cover all tortillas with evenly with sauce.
Spread light layer of cheeses (cheddar and jack) over mixture, sprinkle olives and light coating of parmesan cheese, cover with tortillas and repeat entire process
When filled 1/2" from top of pan-end with loosely placed tortillas and last of cheese

Cover with aluminum foil and bake at 350 degrees for approx 40 minutes or until lightly bubbling on sides.

Cut into squares, scoop out and enjoy

Garnish with sour cream, salsa, and parmesan cheese as optional additions

Laurie Damron – Reader
While the casserole is baking, you can read another chapter in your favorite romance novel.

Chicken and Dressing Casserole

Ingredients:

8 boneless, skinless chicken breasts, stewed
1 can cream of chicken soup
1 can cream of chicken w/mushroom soup
1 cup sour cream
8 oz. Pepperidge Farm herb dressing
1/2 cup melted butter
3/4 cup chicken broth.

Directions:

Butter a 9 x 13 baking dish. Cut chicken into bite-size pieces and place in baking dish. Mix the two soups and sour cream; pour over the chicken.

Top with the herb dressing mix. Drizzle the melted butter over the dressing. Gently spoon the chicken broth over the dressing.

Bake at 350 degrees for one hour or until top is browned.

Allie Boniface
www.allieboniface.com

Tomato Company Cups
(originally appeared in *What Can I Bring? Sharing Good Tastes and Times in Northern Virginia*)

Ingredients:

9 bacon slices, cooked and crumbled
1 large tomato, finely chopped
3/4 cup (3 oz.) shredded Swiss cheese
1/2 cup mayonnaise
1 tsp. dried basil
1 (10-ounce) can refrigerated flaky biscuits

Directions:

1. Preheat oven to 375 degrees.
2. Combine first five ingredients.
3. Separate each biscuit into 2 or 3 thinner ones. Press the biscuit pieces into muffin pan cups, layering to make shells.
4. Fill the biscuit shells evenly with the tomato mixture.
5. Bake at 375 degrees for 10 to 12 minutes, or until bubbly.

(For a vegetarian variation, substitute green bell pepper for bacon, and sprinkle some freshly grated Parmesan cheese on top.)

Author Note: Since I discovered this recipe, I've made it for appetizers, brunch, lunch, and dinner. I've taken it to baby showers and Super Bowl parties. I've served it to my in-laws, my real estate broker, my co-workers, and my husband (who requests it almost weekly). Without fail, people ask me for the recipe; now I just keep extra copies on hand. It's super-easy and can be modified for the vegetarians in your life too. Enjoy!

Paige Cuccaro
www.paigecuccaro.com
www.alisonpaige.net

Sicilian Meat Roll

Ingredients:

2 eggs, beaten
3/4 cup soft bread crumbs
1/2 cup tomato juice
2 tbsp. parsley flakes
1/2 tsp. dried oregano, crushed
1 small clove garlic, minced
2 lb. lean ground beef
8 slices thin boiled ham
1 1/2 cup shredded Mozzarella cheese
3 slices Mozzarella cheese

Combine first 6 ingredients and:
1/4 tsp. salt
1/4 tsp. pepper

Directions:

Add beef; mix well
On foil, pat meat to 12 x 10 inch rectangle. Arrange ham on top. Top with shredded cheese.
Starting from the short end, carefully roll up meat, using foil to lift; seal edges and ends.
Place seam side down in a 13 x 9 x 2-inch baking pan; bake at 350 degree in oven for an hour and fifteen minutes.
Halve cheese diagonally; place on top of roll. Return to oven until cheese is melted.

Serves 8

Nancy Warren
www.nancywarren.net

Chicken with Mandarin Oranges & Almonds

Ingredients:

2 oz. seedless raisins
1 jigger Madeira (I use port)
2 tsp. paprika
1 tsp. white pepper
1 free range chicken 3.1/2 to 4 lbs. (or chicken breasts, 1/2 breast per person)
5 tbsp. oil
1 can mandarin oranges (probably could fresh oranges, I've never tried them)
1 clove garlic minced
1/2 cup hot beef bouillon
1 tbsp. cornstarch
1 tbsp. soy sauce
1 tsp. finely chopped ginger (can use powdered)
1/2 cup heavy cream lightly beaten
1 tbsp. butter
2 tbsp. sliced almonds

Cover raisins with Madeira (or whatever) and soak overnight

Mix together paprika and pepper, rub chicken with mixture. Heat oil in skillet, add chicken and fry until golden on all sides, about 10 minutes. Drain oranges, reserve juice. Measure 1/2 cup juice, pour over chicken, add garlic, pour in bouillon, cover. Simmer chicken in skillet 30 minutes, or bake in 325 degree oven until chicken is cooked. Add raisins, cook 5 minutes.

Remove chicken with slotted spoon, arrange on preheated platter, keep warm. Blend cornstarch with small amount cold water, add to sauce in pan, stir until thickened, season with soy sauce and ginger. Add oranges and cream, heat through but do not boil. Heat butter in small skillet, add sliced almonds, cook until golden. Pour sauce over chicken, top with almonds. Serves six.

Aaron Foster, Lori Foster's oldest son

This was always a quick and healthy meal to put together when Mom was too busy writing to cook.

Turkey Chili

Ingredients:

1 lb. ground turkey
2 packets fajita seasoning
2 cans black beans
2 cans corn
1 can stewed diced tomatoes
1 can tomato juice

Directions:

Brown turkey in a large pot.
Add seasonings, stirring to mix.
Add remaining ingredients.
Allow to boil down to desired consistency, then serve.

Amber Green
www.shapeshiftersinlust.com

Baby Back Ribs

Ingredients:

1 cup water or apple juice (or mix)
1 cup apple cider vinegar
Salt and pepper
2 strong onions, sliced thin
2 full or 3 trimmed racks baby back ribs (total under 5 lbs)
1 cup mustard-based commercial barbecue sauce
3 oz. frozen orange juice concentrate
1 shot glass of coffee
1 tsp. minced or crushed ginger
1 tsp. minced or crushed garlic
2-3 good hard splashes hot pepper sauce
double-handful chipped or chopped pecan wood, soaked in water

Directions:

Preheat oven to 325 degrees.

Cut each rack of ribs in half or in thirds.

Place ribs in enamel Dutch oven, salting and peppering each layer and putting generous layer of onion slices between each layer of meat. Do not cram the ribs in too tight—if you have a half-rack that won't fit in without mashing, set it aside for another day. Pour water/apple juice and vinegar over top of meat stack.

Cover and bake an hour and a quarter, turning after first 35 minutes and then every 20 minutes to change out which ribs are on bottom and in the middle. Don't try to keep the onions where they belong in the layers; just keep them in the pan.

Meanwhile, stir everything else (except wood chips) together and simmer for half an hour, then cut off the heat and let the sauce rest until the meat is ready.

Bring grill to medium heat and add the chips.

Spray or lightly grease grillwork. Grill meat in the smoke over medium heat for 15 minutes, turning once. (Throw away vinegar/onion mix, or feed to your chickens.)

When each side of meat has had 7-8 minutes facing down, baste ribs with barbecue sauce. Grill another 7-8 minutes. Turn, baste again with barbecue sauce, and grill a final 7-8 minutes.

Indoors variation:

Sprinkle the ribs with liquid smoke before the liquid cooking, and mix a tbsp. of liquid smoke into the sauce. Instead of grilling, broil the ribs to caramelize the exterior.

Debby Conrad
www.debbyconrad.com

Chicken and Cream Cheese Crescents

Ingredients:

2 cups cooked chicken, diced or shredded
1 pkg. cream cheese, softened
3 tbsp. milk
1/2 tsp. minced dried onions or onion powder
Salt and pepper to taste

Directions:

Mix above ingredients together.

Unroll 2 packages of Pillsbury crescent rolls. Use 2 triangles and pinch seams together to make a square. Top each square with a scoop of the chicken mixture. Then take the 4 corners of each crescent and pull to the center. Pinch seams to close each one. Place on cookie sheets. Brush each square with melted butter and sprinkle crushed seasoned croutons on top.

Bake at 350 degrees until golden brown. (About 20-30 min) Serve with your favorite veggie and a side of cranberry sauce for color.

Dawn Seewer – Creative Services
www.dagiancreative.com

Chicken Marsala

Ingredients:

4 skinless, boneless, chicken breasts (about 1 1/2 lbs.)
All-purpose flour, for dredging
Salt and freshly ground black pepper
1/4 cup extra-virgin olive oil
4 oz. prosciutto, thinly sliced
Handful of sliced mushrooms
1/2 cup sweet Marsala wine
1/2 cup chicken stock
2 tbsp. unsalted butter
1/4 cup heavy cream

Directions:

Flatten chicken with mallet, until they are about 1/4-inch thick. Put some flour in a shallow dish and season with a fair amount of salt and pepper.

Heat the oil over medium-high flame in a large skillet. When the oil is nice and hot, dredge both sides of the chicken in the seasoned flour, shaking off the excess. Fry for dredged chicken breasts on each side until golden, turning once. Take chicken out of the pan and set aside for a moment.

Lower the heat to medium and add the prosciutto to the drippings in the pan, sauté for 1 minute to render out some of the fat. Now, add the mushrooms and sauté until they are nicely browned and their moisture has evaporated, about 5 minutes; season with salt and pepper. Pour the Marsala in the pan and boil down for a few seconds to cook out the alcohol. Add the chicken stock and simmer for a minute to reduce the sauce slightly. Stir in the butter and return the chicken to the pan; simmer gently for about 15 minutes or until chicken is cooked through. Remove chicken, add the cream and cook sauce until thick enough to coat the back of a spoon. Season to taste and spoon over chicken.

Lori Foster
www.lorifoster.com

Easy Italian Chicken

Ingredients:

1 pkg. skinless, boneless chicken breasts
1 bottle Wishbone Italian dressing
salt and pepper
melted butter

Directions:

Preheat oven to 425 degrees.
Lay out chicken on a lined baking sheet. (Use a sheet with edges – it will drip)
Brush tops of chicken with melted butter.
Sprinkle generously with dressing
Salt and pepper

Cook 20 minutes, turn, repeat all of the above and cook at least another 20 minutes, or until desired doneness.

Author Note:

You can also do this easy chicken recipe on the grill. Just wrap the chicken in aluminum foil and turn the foil packages several times to avoid burning. The dressing might blacken where it drips off the chicken and onto the pan.

Lori Foster
www.lorifoster.com

Oven-fried Chicken

Ingredients:

1 pkg. skinless, boneless chicken
1 stick margarine or butter
Package of crackers
1 tbsp. Poultry seasoning
1 tsp. Salt
1 tsp. Pepper
Egg, cracked and mixed with 1/3 cup water.

Directions:

Preheat the over to 400 degrees.
Put the stick of butter in a foiled lined baking pan and put in oven to melt.
Meanwhile, put crackers and seasonings into a zip top plastic bag and using a rolling pin, crush crackers finely.

Dip each piece of chicken into the water/egg mixture, then drop into cracker bag. Shake the pieces to get them thoroughly coated.
Lay them in the sizzling melted butter.
Bake 1/2 hour on each side, then test for doneness. Can cook for up to another 1/2 hour, depending of sizes of chicken pieces.

Author Note:

You can also use a regular cut-up chicken with skin if you prefer.

Suzanne Forster
www.suzanneforster.com

"Hot Stuff" Tamale Pie

Ingredients:

1 tbsp. shortening
1 medium onion, chopped (about 1/2 cup)
1 can (15 oz.) pork tamales in sauce
1 can (15 oz.) whole kernel corn
1 can (8 oz.) tomato sauce
1 tsp. chili powder
Cayenne powder to taste
1 cup shredded sharp Cheddar cheese (about 4 oz.)
1/4 cup sliced pitted black olives

Directions:

Heat oven to 350 degrees. Melt shortening in medium skillet. Add onion; cook and stir until tender. Drain sauce from tamales; stir sauce, com (with liquid), tomato sauce and chili powder into skillet. Season with cayenne powder for a hotter, spicy pie. Simmer uncovered 5 minutes.

Pour into ungreased square pan, 9x9x2 inches. Stir in half the cheese. Remove papers from tamales, arrange them spoke fashion in pan. Sprinkle olives and remaining cheese in center. Cover; bake 15 minutes and enjoy. But have an ice-cold drink handy. It's quick, taste and hot. Ole!

Kathy Andrico – Reader

"Reading a Sophie Metropolis mystery by Tori Carrington makes me reminiscent of when I was younger and the great Greek food my aunts and uncles made."

Yiayia's Keftethes
Greek Garlic Burgers
Or Greek Meatballs

Ingredients:

3-4" ground round beef
1 egg beaten
2 pieces lightly toasted bread
1 onion
1-2 cloves garlic (to taste)
salt & pepper (to taste)
1 tsp. cinnamon

Directions:

Finely dice the onion. Then towel dry. Set aside.
Finely dice the garlic (or press). Set aside.
Soak the lightly toasted bread in milk. Squeeze out the extra milk.

In mixing bowl, add the beef, egg and toast. Mix by hand. Add the onion, garlic, salt, pepper & cinnamon. Thoroughly mix.

Put olive oil in skillet. Make small burger patties and dip each side in flour. Cook slowly at medium heat.

J.C. Wilder / Dominique Adair
www.jcwilder.com / www.dominiqueadair.com

Asian Orange Chicken

Ingredients:

Sauce:

1 1/2 cups water
2 tbsp. orange juice
1/4 cup lemon juice
1/3 cup rice vinegar
2 1/2 tbsp. soy sauce
1 tbsp. grated orange zest
1 cup packed brown sugar
1/2 tsp. minced fresh ginger root
1/2 tsp. minced garlic
2 tbsp. chopped green onion
1/4 tsp. red pepper flakes
3 tbsp. cornstarch
2 tbsp. water

Chicken:

2 boneless, skinless chicken breasts, cut into 1/2 inch pieces
1 cup all-purpose flour
1/4 tsp. salt
1/4 tsp. pepper
3 tbsp. olive oil

Directions:

Pour into saucepan 1 1/2 cups water, orange juice, lemon juice, rice vinegar, and soy sauce; and set over medium-high heat. Stir in orange zest, brown sugar, ginger, garlic, and chopped onion. Bring to a boil. Remove from heat, and let cool 10 to 15 minutes.

Place chicken pieces into a resealable plastic bag. When contents of saucepan have cooled, pour 1 cup of sauce into bag. Reserve remaining sauce. Seal bag, and refrigerate at least 2 hours.

In another resealable plastic bag, mix the flour, salt, and pepper. Add marinated chicken pieces, and shake to coat.

Heat the oil in a large skillet over medium heat. Place chicken in skillet, and brown on both sides. Remove to paper towels, and cover with aluminum foil.

Wipe out the skillet, and add the sauce. Bring to a boil over medium-high heat. Mix together cornstarch and 2 tbsp. water, and stir into sauce. Reduce heat to medium low; stir in chicken pieces, and simmer, about 5 minutes, stirring occasionally.

Shana Schwer – Reader
This is an easy quick meal for when I'm chapters-deep
into the newest Lori Foster novel!

Spaghetti Pizza

Ingredients: Base

16 oz. spaghetti
2 eggs
1/2 cup milk
1 cup mozzarella-shredded
3/4 tsp. garlic powder

Top:

30-32 oz. pizza sauce*
1 1/2 tsp. oregano
3 cups shredded mozzarella
1-3 1/2 oz. pkg. pepperoni
Hamburger or Italian sausage to taste

* Ragu can be used, or your favorite home made sauce

Directions:

Break spaghetti into 2 inch pieces. Cook 8 minutes, drain
and cool. Heat oven to 400 degrees. In large bowl beat eggs
slightly and add other "base" ingredients. Stir well, add
spaghetti and mix till well coated. Spread in greased jelly roll
pan and pat down. Bake 15 minutes. Remove and reduce heat
to 350 degrees. Spread sauce over evenly, sprinkle with
oregano, add cheese and pepperoni. Bake 30 minutes. Let stand
5 minutes before cutting.

Vina Foster, Lori Foster's mother in law

Easy Chicken Pot Pie

Ingredients:

1 2/3 cup frozen mixed vegetables, thawed
1 cup cut up cooked chicken
1 can (10 3/4 oz.) condensed cream of chicken soup
1 cup Bisquick Original or Reduced Fat baking mix
1/2 cup milk
1 egg

Heat oven to 400 degrees.
Mix vegetables, chicken and soup in ungreased 9" pie plate
Bake 3 minutes or until gold brown.
Makes 6 servings

Laurie Damron – Reader
This is the perfect tasty blend of ingredients, just like
a Janice Maynard novel.

Hash Brown Casserole

Ingredients:

1 - 2 lb. pkg. frozen hash browns
16 oz. sour cream
1 can cream of chicken soup
1 stick butter, melted
1/2 cup chopped onion
2 cups grated cheddar cheese

Mix all ingredients, spread into 13" x 9" pan and bake at
350 degrees for 45 minutes.

Tilly Greene
www.tillygreene.com

Recipe for Poor Man Tacos

Ingredients:

1 lb. ground beef
5 large potatoes
10 large carrots
salt and pepper
24 corn tortillas
Corn or Sunflower Oil

Directions

Filling:

Peel and quarter the potatoes. Peel and chop the carrots. Place both potatoes and carrots into a pot of boiling water, put the lid on, and boil until soft [you can put a fork in them and they slide right off].

While the above is boiling, chop, slice and dice the accompaniments [see below for suggestions], put them in separate dishes and place on the table. Also, before the above finishes boiling, get out a skillet, and brown the beef, seasoning with salt and pepper to taste. Once cooked, drain the all the grease out.

When the potatoes and carrots are boiled, drain all the water out then mash both together. Doesn't have to be smooth perfect, lumpy is just fine. Next, stir in beef.

Tacos:

Put a clean skillet on the stove, add oil [yes, there's lots of the stuff, pour to cover bottom of the pan by about a 1/4 inch], heat and keep heated at a medium to medium-high, until the last taco is fried.

This part is fast paced so be ready. Using tongs, place a corn tortilla in the oil, fry for 15 seconds, turn over, add two heaping spoons of filling on one half, then bring the other half over to cover [now you see the taco shape ☺]. Flip the taco over after about 1 to 1 1/2 minutes [don't want it to burn just get hard], and cook same amount of time. When finished, take out of skillet using tongs, allow as much of the oil as you can to drip off and then place on a plate covered with paper towels to absorb more oil. A normal sized skillet will allow you to cook 2 tacos at a time and takes about 15 minutes to do up all 24— yes, it's a quick meal to make once everything is prepared [filling can be made days in advance if you'd like].

When they are all done cooking, take out to the table and enjoy. Allow your diners to choose what they want to put in their taco. Here are a few suggestions:

Grated cheese [I suggest Colby for easy melting]
Sliced lettuce [iceberg is best]
Chopped tomatoes, avocadoes, green onions, and cilantro
Salsa and hot sauce
Sour Cream

Author Note:

Poor Man Tacos have been a staple in my family since before I was born. My Grandfather was the Chief in a downtown Los Angeles fire department and my Grandma used to cook for the crew. Amongst other things, tacos were one of the easiest and quickest dishes to make, that also passed the "call away" test...tasted wonderful hot from the kitchen, but also when they returned from a fire. Using vegetables meant not as much meat was necessary and hence the "poor man". Traditionally cabbage and mayonnaise were the only things added but as time has moved on, my family has made a little advancement with the "fixings" area. Personally my favorite way to eat poor man tacos [you never have just one] is with cheese, cabbage and mayo. Thankfully they are always on the menu when I go to moms, and yes, I've even bagged some up and stuck them in my luggage to eat when I get home.

Gabriella Hewitt
www.gabriellahewitt.com

Arroz Con Pollo
(Chicken with Rice)
Cook Time: 45 minutes

Preheat oven to 350 degrees
Serves 8

Ingredients:
1 cup Long Grain Enriched Rice
4 cloves garlic chopped
1 large Spanish or yellow onion chopped
Olive oil
2 lbs. Chicken legs and thighs
Baby Carrots
Tumeric seeds (pinch)
Salt & pepper (for taste)
1 Goya Saffron packet
1 cube or packet Chicken Bouillon
2 cups water
1 cup dry white wine

Directions:

In a large pot or skillet pour olive oil with just enough to coat bottom of pan. Add in chopped onion and garlic. Put in a dash of turmeric for flavor. Add in Saffron packet and stir. Cook till the onions become yellow and soft. Salt & pepper chicken to taste. Place chicken inside the pan and lightly brown chicken on both sides. Pour in dry white. Bring to a boil. Mix in chicken bouillon into water. Reduce heat and add in bouillon water. Cook for 15 minutes.

In a separate baking dish, pour the rice and evenly spread until bottom is covered. Take the chicken out of the pan and arrange on top of the rice. Then slowly pour the hot sauce from the pan into the baking dish. Place carrots in between the chicken making sure to immersed carrots in the sauce. Cover with aluminum foil.

Cook for 30 minutes or until rice is soft and tender. Chicken should be thoroughly cooked through to the bone.

QUICK and EASY Recipe

Rice:

Pour rice into a rice cooker. Add Saffron packet and water. Put diced frozen carrots and peas.

Chicken breasts sliced thin, season with onion and garlic powder. Salt and pepper to taste. In a skillet coat bottom with olive oil, brown chicken breasts on both sides. Add in dry white wine and chicken bouillon water. Bring to a boil and reduce heat. Let it cook for 10 minutes.

Serve chicken and sauce over rice.

Excitement. **S**uspense. **P**assion. *Sabor!* Come taste the tropical flavor of Puerto Rico and get swept up in the intrigue and passion of the island's Dark Waters.

Dark Waters, a romantic suspense release in Fall 2007 by debut author Gabriella Hewitt.

Visit Gabriella Hewitt at www.gabriellahewitt.com and find more Puerto Rican recipes.

Desserts

Stella Cameron
www.stellacameron.com

Oranges Cointreau

Ingredients:

6 large oranges
Vanilla bean ice cream
Orange sherbet
Jelly of choice
Cointreau (or Triple Sec—it's cheaper)

Meringue Topping

4 egg whites
Pinch cream of tartar
1/2 cup sugar

Brandy

Directions:

Slice off enough of bottoms of oranges to make them balance on a platter. Slice off tops of oranges and take out pulp. Line insides of oranges with vanilla ice cream around 1/2" thick. Put a small amount of jelly and Cointreau (or Triple Sec) at the inner bottoms. Fill rest of space with orange sherbet. Freeze until you're ready to serve.

Egg whites and cream of tartar should be beaten stiff, then sugar added slowly and whole mixture beaten stiff again. Heap meringue on top of oranges and be careful to seal off the ice cream/sherbet filling. Evenly space oranges on knock-em-dead platter, warm the brandy a bit, set it on fire and pour over oranges at the table.

This dessert is guaranteed to bring a giant chorus of, "Ooh!" and really finishes things off nicely when served following my favorite Zeek's Green Froggy pizza. Do check on how much time to allow for pizza delivery and don't light the brandy for the oranges too soon. Remove pizza box from table before setting brandy afire.

Ingela F. Hyatt
www.IngelaHyatt.com

Ingela's Scrumptious Raisin & Pecan Cookies

Ingredients:

1/2 cup shortening
1/2 cup sugar
1 egg
1 tsp. vanilla
1 cup sifted all-purpose flour
1 tsp. baking soda
dash of salt
1/2 tsp. cinnamon
1/2 tsp. ginger
1/2 tsp. ground cloves
1/2 cup raisins
1/4 cup pecans (finely chopped)

Directions:

Cream shortening, sugar, vanilla, and egg together till light and fluffy. Sift dry ingredients together; stir into creamed mixture. Add raisins and finely chopped pecans to dough and stir. Drop onto lightly greased cookie sheet approximately 2 inches apart. Bake at 375 degree for 7 to 8 minutes. Makes 3 dozen.

Note from author: Believe it or not, I created these cookies when was just eight years old. I loved cookies and cooking as a kid and wanted to create my very own recipe. So my mom and I sat at the kitchen table one rainy afternoon. She held up the various spices and possible ingredients, and I choose what I thought sounded good. Then we put it all together, and were surprised to find I'd come up with a very tasty recipe. Since then I have made many more recipes, and enjoy throwing something together on the spot for lunch or dinner. I hope you enjoy these great cookies, and they become a family favorite as they have with mine.

Lori Foster
www.lorifoster.com

White Chocolate Cake

Set the oven at 350 degrees. Oil and flour two 9" round cake pans

Ingredients:

3/4 to 1 lb. of white chocolate, 1/2 and 1/2
1 cup butter
3/4 cup buttermilk
2 cups sugar
1 cup powdered sugar, give or take (for frosting)
4 eggs, separated
1 tsp. vanilla
2 1/2 cup flour
1 tsp. baking powder
1 cup chopped pecans
1 cup coconut

Directions:

Cream together butter, sugar and egg yolks; add vanilla and mix; add half of melted white chocolate (cooled) and mix. Mix together baking powder and flour; add to the butter, sugar, egg yolks mixture until smooth alternately add in the buttermilk, egg whites, pecans and coconut. Bake for 45 minutes to 1 hour, until toothpick inserted in center comes out clean.

NOTE: cake is *very* heavy and won't rise much at all. Remove cakes from oven and let cool.

Melt remaining white chocolate, let cool, then add in powdered sugar (and maybe a few teaspoons of milk) until smooth spreading consistency. Frost cake. Enjoy!

Allie Mackay
www.alliemackay.com

Cranachan
(A Festive Scottish Dessert)

Ingredients:

1 pint heavy whipping cream
3 tbsp. honey (heather honey if you can find some)
3 tbsp. **whisky
4 tbsp. thick, plain yoghurt
2 tbsp. oatmeal (you can add 2 tbsp. slivered almonds if you wish)
1 cup fresh raspberries

Directions:

Lightly toast the oatmeal (and slivered almonds) on a cookie sheet in the oven until golden. Set aside to cool. Put the whipping cream, honey, and whisky in a mixing bowl and whip until peaks form. Now fold in the yoghurt and then spoon the mixture into a pretty serving dish and chill for 2 to 3 hours. Before serving, sprinkle the golden-toasted oatmeal (and slivered almonds) over the Cranachan and pile the fresh raspberries in the center.

This recipe should serve 4 to 6.

**apple juice can be substituted for the whisky, but the real thing is better and more authentic.

Holly Fitzgerald

Heavenly Berry Gelato
Holly Fitzgerald's award-winning combination

Ingredients:

2 cups milk or heavy cream
1/2 tsp. grated lemon peel
4 yolks
1/2 cup sugar
1/8 tsp. salt
1/2 pint of blueberries
1/2 pint of raspberries
1/2 pint of strawberries
1 cup of melted chocolate chips

Directions:

In a saucepan, heat the milk and lemon peel to a simmer then turn off the heat and allow to infuse 10 minutes. Meanwhile, whisk the yolks with the sugar and salt till very light in color and fluffy. Whisk in the hot milk and return the mixture to the heat. Add chocolate chips, stirring until melted. Cook carefully until it thickens then remove from heat. Pour the custard base into a new container add berries and cool it in an ice bath. Turn as per manufacturer's instructions.

Dianne Castell
www.DianneCastell.com

Pecan Pie

Ingredients:

9" unbaked pie crust
1 cup light corn syrup
1 cup firmly packed dark brown sugar
3 eggs slightly beaten
1/3 cut butter melted
1/2 tsp. salt
1 tsp. vanilla
1 cup pecan halves (or walnuts)

Directions:

Heat over to 350 degree. Combine corn syrup, sugar, eggs, butter, salt, vanilla and mix well. Pour into crust, sprinkle with nuts and bake for 50 min till knife comes out clean. Cool. Add whipped cream, ice cream etc.

Becky Barker
www.beckybarker.com

Cinnamon Sweet Rolls

Ingredients & Directions:

18-20 frozen bread rolls1 package butterscotch pudding (not instant)
10 -12 pecan halves

Spray bundt cake pan with non-stick spray and dust it with some of the pudding powder. Place pecan halves upside down along the bottom of the pan and then put the rolls on top. Sprinkle the rest of the pudding powder over the rolls. Then mix the syrup:

3/4 cup of brown sugar
1/2 cup of butter (1 stick)
3/4 tsp. of cinnamon
1/2 cup of chopped pecans (optional)

Bring syrup to bubbly boil and then pour over the rolls, cover lightly with foil. (I spray the foil with non-stick spray, too) Let rise for a few hours or overnight. Bake at 350 degrees for about 30 minutes. Let cool slightly (2-3 minutes) and then turn out of the pan onto a very large plate. Extremely hot and sticky, so use caution. Yummy!

Note: Some people call these sticky buns or monkey bread. This recipe is so easy and the rolls look beautiful when they're done. People will think you slaved for hours!

Ann M. Warner

www.annwarner.com

Little Grandma's Brownies

Ingredients:

1 1/2 squares unsweetened chocolate
1/2 cup shortening: can be all butter, or half butter, half
olive oil
1 cup white sugar
1/4 tsp. salt
2 eggs
1/2 cup flour
2/3 cup nuts (walnuts or pecans)
1 tsp. vanilla

Directions:

Melt the chocolate and butter (microwave or double-boiler). Add salt, sugar, eggs, flour nuts and vanilla. Bake at 325 degrees. Do not overcook. Best when still just a little gooey.
Note: This is a treasured recipe from my grandmother.

Ann M. Warner

www.annwarner.com

Chocolate or Grand Marnier Soufflé

Ingredients & Directions:

STEP 1. The pudding This part can be done ahead, a day, or more. Separate 6 eggs. Reserve the whites (refrigerate for later). Mix the egg yolks and set aside until Step 3.
1/3 cup flour
1/4 cup sugar

1 1/2 cup milk

Thoroughly mix flour and milk together and strain to remove any lumps. Add sugar and cook mixture in a saucepan over medium heat, stirring, until mixture thickens. Cook 1 min more, and remove from heat.

STEP 2. The Flavoring

A.   FOR A CHOCOLATE SOUFFLE: 1 square of unsweetened chocolate + 1/4 cup chocolate chips, stir until melted.

B.   FOR A GRAND MARNIER SOUFFLE add: 3 tbsp. Grand Marnier + 2 tbsp. low fat butter + 2 tsp. vanilla. Stir well.

STEP 3. The Egg Yolks

Add the 6 egg yolks to the pudding mix. Stir mixture until smooth. Refrigerate pudding mix if not using right away.

STEP 4 Final Assembly

Let the 6 egg whites warm to room temperature then whip at high speed using a mixer. Gradually add:

1/4 tsp. salt

1/4 cup sugar

When the egg whites are stiff and stand in peaks, fold in the pudding mix made in Step 1-2.

Using oil or butter, grease a large soufflé dish or several individual soufflé dishes. After oiling, add sugar to coat the inside of the dish. Spoon in the soufflé mix. Only fill the dish about three-quarters full. Bake 35-40 minutes at 375 degrees until knife inserted in the middle comes out clean. Serve immediately with melted ice cream topping. The soufflé will be very puffy when it first comes out of the oven, then will fall slightly as it cools. In spite of that, left-over soufflé can be refrigerated and is also delicious.

Author Note: This is a decadent, delicious and very romantic dessert, and it's easier to make than you might think!

Kay Stockham
www.kaystockham.com

Lemon Coolers

Ingredients & Directions:

1 box lemon cake mix
1 egg
2 cups whipped topping
powdered sugar
Mix by hand cake mix, whipped topping and egg.
Roll into small balls and roll in powdered sugar.
Place on greased cookie sheet and bake 350 degrees for 8 to 10 minutes.
Cool.

Kay Stockham
www.kaystockham.com

Mom's All-Gone Ice Cream Punch

Ingredients & Directions:

1 large can frozen orange juice (no pulp)
1 - 6 oz. can frozen lemonade
1 cup sugar
1 large can pineapple juice
add water to make one gallon
1 gallon vanilla ice cream
When ready to serve, use ice cream scooper to ball vanilla ice cream in punch bowl, pour punch over top.
FABULOUS!!! Not a strong, citrusy punch but very mild and creamy. Can be made ahead for easy serving.

Jamie Denton
www.jamiedenton.net

Carmel Apple Dip

8 oz. cream cheese, softened
3/4 cup brown sugar firmly packed
2 tbsp. vanilla
8 to 10 apples thinly sliced (for Christmas I use red and green apples)

Combine first three ingredients and stir until smooth. Store in refrigerator in a covered container.

At least 2 hours before serving, bring to room temperature, or heat in microwave for about 1 minute and serve warm. Use sliced apples for dipping. Yum!

Roseanne Dowell
www.roseannedowell.com

Lorna Dune Low Cal Pudding Cake

1 3/4 cup cold fat free half and half
1 pkg. (4 serving size) sugar free instant pudding, any kind
24 Voortman sugar free shortbread swirls
1 banana sliced
2 cups light cool whip

Pour half and half and pudding into bowl. Beat with a wire whisk for 2 min. or until well blended. Let stand for 5 minutes. Arrange 1/2 the cookies in a 1 1/2 quart casserole. Cover with 1/2 each of pudding, banana, and cool whip. Refrigerate for 3 hours before serving. Store in refrigerator. Serves 8

Jamie Denton
www.jamiedenton.net

Strawberry Cheat Cake

Ingredients:

1 White Cake Mix
2 Cans Comstock (or equivalent) Strawberry Pie Filling
1 8 oz. pkg. Cream cheese

Directions:

Mix and bake white cake mix according to package directions in a 9×13 oblong baking dish. Let cool completely.

Use about 1 tbsp. of the juice from the pie filling and mix with cream cheese. (Note: I've never tried it, but you could probably "cheat" and use the Philadelphia brand strawberry cream cheese and skip this step.)

Evenly spread cream cheese over cooled cake to about 1/4"? from the edge. Spread 2 cans of strawberry pie filling on top.*

Chill for a minimum of 2 hours and enjoy! Store any leftovers in fridge.

*Note: During strawberry season, I exchange the canned pie filling for 4 cups fresh quartered strawberries mixed with strawberry glaze, but that's more work and not exactly cheating. Also, for large parties, simply double the recipe by using two boxes of white cake mix, then bake in a large, half-sheet cake pan.

Heather Grothaus
www.HeatherGrothaus.com

Milk Chocolate Brownies

This is a super-easy recipe for delicious and pretty brownies from scratch! You might never use a mix again!

Ingredients:

1/2 cup butter (1 stick)
2 cup sugar
4 eggs
2 tsp. vanilla
1 1/2 cup flour
1/2 cup cocoa
1/2 tsp. salt
1/2 cup chocolate chips (I've also used M&M's!)
2 tbsp. sugar
1/2 cup chopped walnuts

Directions:

Melt butter in a heavy, medium-sized sauce pan over low heat. Remove from heat. Add sugar and mix well. Stir in eggs and vanilla until blended. Stir together flour, cocoa and salt, add to sugar mixture and mix well. Spread in a greased (or sprayed) 9" x 13" baking dish. Sprinkle chocolate chips, nuts and sugar over batter and bake at 350 degrees for 25 minutes.

Donna MacMeans
www.DonnaMacMeans.com

Fuzzy Naval Cake

We do a lot of tailgating here in Columbus, Ohio. By far, this is my most requested recipe for tailgating and any kind of adult gathering. The center is extremely moist and potent. Be warned—this cake can give you a bit of a buzz.

Ingredients:

1 box yellow cake mix
1/2 cup vegetable oil
2 pkgs. instant vanilla pudding (6 oz total)
4 eggs
1 cup Peach Schnapps, divided
1/2 cup and 2 Tbsps orange juice
1/2 tsp. orange extract
1 cup confectioner's sugar

Directions:

Preheat oven to 350 degrees. Grease & flour a bundt pan (I use a baker's spray myself)

Beat cake mix, oil, dry pudding mix, eggs, 3/4 cup of schnapps, 1/2 cup of orange juice and orange extract all together. Pour into the bundt pan and bake for 45-50 min.
Remove pan from the oven but do not un-mold the cake.

While the cake is still hot, combine in a small bowl: 1/4 cup of Peach schnapps, 2 tbsp. of orange juice and confectioner's sugar. Stir until blended. Poke holes in the top of the warm cake. Carefully spoon the sugar mixture over the top of the cake until it has all been absorbed into the center of the cake. Let the cake cook for another two hours. Turn it out of the mold.

Liz Andrews
www.lizandrews.net

Triple Chocolate Decadence Cake

Ingredients:

1 pkg. Chocolate Cake Mix
1 small box chocolate pudding (instant)
2 cups sour cream
4 eggs
3/4 cups oil
1/2 cup Kalua (water or milk can be substituted)
12 oz. bag chocolate chips

Directions:

Mix all ingredients together in a bowl, folding in the chocolate chips at the very end once most everything else is mixed. Pour into a greased and floured bundt pan and bake a 350 degrees for one hour. Once cool, invert cake and sprinkle with powdered sugar.

Slice and enjoy.

Celine Chatillon
www.celinechatillon.com

Pumpkin Pie Bars

(This recipe works well with fresh pumpkin, too.)

Ingredients:

1 (18 1/2 oz.) box yellow cake mix
1/2 cup melted margarine
4 eggs
1 30 oz. can pumpkin (can use about four cups fresh pumpkin)
1 cup sugar, divided
1/2 cup brown sugar
2/3 evaporated milk
1 1/2 tsp. cinnamon
1/2 cup chopped walnuts
1/4 cup softened margarine

Directions:

Preheat oven to 350 degrees. Spray a 13 X 9 " pan.
Remove 1 cup of cake mix and set aside.
Beat 1 egg. In large bowl, stir together remaining cake mix, melted butter and beaten egg. Press into pan.
Beat remaining 3 eggs and stir in pumpkin, 1/2 cup white sugar, brown sugar, milk and cinnamon. Pour over cake mixture in pan.
To the remaining cake mix add 1/2 cup white sugar, walnuts and softened margarine. Mix till crumbly and sprinkle on top.
Bake for 35 minutes or until knife comes out clean in center.

Cynthianna Appel
www.cynthianna.com

The Food of the Gods

2 to 3 medium navel oranges, peeled and cut into bite-sized
    pieces
1 cup (or more) shredded, sweetened coconut
1 can of pineapple chunks, drained
1 to 2 medium bananas, sliced in bite-sized pieces
Candied maraschino cherries, halved

Mix all ingredients except cherries in a salad bowl. Top with a circle of halved cherries and extra coconut if desired. Cover and chill until serving. Enjoy!

Catherine Mann
www.CatherineMann.com

Boiled Cocoa Cookies

2 cups sugar
1 stick butter/margarine
1/4 cup cocoa
1/2 cup milk
1 tsp. vanilla
1/2 cup peanut butter
2 1/2 cups oatmeal
1 cup nuts(optional)

Mix and boil sugar, butter/margarine, cocoa & milk for 2 minutes, stir frequently. Remove from heat, add vanilla, peanut butter, oatmeal & nuts. Mix well. Spoon by spoonfuls onto wax paper.
    *Work quickly as mix will start to thicken in a hurry.

Catherine Mann
www.CatherineMann.com

Strawberry Cake

Ingredients:

1 box white cake mix
1 (3 oz. pkg.) strawberry Jello
1 cup vegetable oil
4 eggs
1/2 cup water
1 (16 ounce pkg.) frozen strawberries (Let thaw before using
   and reserve 1/2 cup juice for frosting.)

Directions:

Preheat oven to 350 degrees. Dump all ingredients into a large bowl. Mix well. Pour into 3 un-greased cake pans. Bake at 350 degrees for 30-35 minutes. Let cool before frosting.

Frosting:
1 box powdered sugar
1/2 cup margarine
1/2 cup strawberry juice

Diane Whiteside
www.DianeWhiteside.com

Brandy Brownies

Ingredients:

2 oz. bittersweet chocolate
1 cup butter
3/4 cup packed dark brown sugar
2 eggs
2 tbsp. cognac (or brandy)
1 tbsp. vanilla
1/4 cup instant espresso (or instant coffee)
1-1/2 cups flour
1/2 tsp. salt
1 tsp. baking soda
1 cup chocolate chips
1 cup coarsely chopped hazelnuts (or walnuts)

Directions:

Preheat oven to 350 degrees. Grease two 8x8 inch pans.
In a double boiler, over hot water, melt chocolate. (Or melt it in a microwave oven.)
In a large mixing bowl, cream together butter and sugar. Add eggs, cognac and vanilla. Mix until smooth, then add chocolate, instant coffee, flour, salt and soda. Fold chocolate chips and hazelnuts into flour mixture.
Spread batter into pans. Bake for 15-20 minutes or until edges are set and middle jiggles. Do not over bake; the brownies will be moist.

NOTE: You can really taste the quality of the chocolate and the cognac in this recipe. I try to buy the best available – Ghirardelli, Guittard, Callebaut, Courvoisier, etc. – and use any leftovers to inspire the chef and the chef's family.
Enjoy!

Kathleen Lawless
www.kathleenlawless.com

Perfect to nibble on while reading your favorite romance novel!

Tiger Butter

Ingredients:

1/2 lb. white chocolate
1/2 cup smooth peanut butter
1/2 cup semi-sweet chocolate

Directions:

Line a 9" square pan with wax paper.
Melt the white chocolate and peanut butter and smooth into the pan.
(this can be done in a double boiler or the microwave)
Melt the semi-sweet chocolate
Swirl it through the white chocolate and the peanut butter for a marbled effect.
Chill or freeze, and cut into squares

Author Note:

A small tin of this makes a great hostels gift.

Jodi Lynn Copeland
www.JodiLynnCopeland.com

Éclair Dessert Cake

Ingredients:

1 large box of vanilla pudding
3 cups of cold milk
1 box of graham crackers
1 (12 oz.) container of whipped topping (i.e. Cool Whip)
1 bottle of hardening chocolate (i.e. Magic Shell)

Directions:

In a medium-sized bowl, mix pudding with milk until thick. Set aside for 5 minutes, and then combine the pudding mixture with whipped topping. Butter the bottom of a 9x13 pan. Put in a single layer of graham crackers and 1/2 of the pudding mixture. Add another layer of graham crackers, and the rest of the pudding mixture. Add a final layer of graham crackers, and pour hardening chocolate over top. Chill covered in the refrigerator for 12-24 hours before serving.

Denysé Bridger
denysebridger.com

Old-Fashioned Plain Cake

Ingredients & Directions:

2 cups white sugar
1 cup butter, margarine, or shortening, whatever is your
  preference
Cream together until light and fluffy, then add:
4 eggs
1 tsp. vanilla, or favorite flavoring

Sift together:
3 cups flour
3 tsp. baking powder
1 tsp. salt

Also needed:
1 cup milk

Add half the dry ingredients to the butter mixture, with half
the milk, blend until smooth. Then repeat with remaining dry
ingredients and milk.

Bake at 350 degrees for one hour.

For chocolate cake, substitute 1/2 cup cocoa for 1/2 cup of
flour.

This is an old recipe, but it makes one of the nicest cakes
you're ever likely to eat! It's simple and easy, but very tasty!!

Cindy Cruciger
www.CindyCruciger.com

Santa's Whiskers

Ingredients:

1 cup butter
1 cup sugar
2 tbsp. heavy whipping cream
1 tbsp. of almond extract
2 1/2 cups all-purpose flour
3/4 cup chopped red or green candied cherries and\or pineapple
1/2 cup slivered almonds
standard bag (12 ozs or more) of flaked coconut
diced almond paste (optional)

Directions:

Cream together butter and sugar; blend in cream, vanilla and almond extract. Stir in remaining ingredients (all but the coconut) beginning with the flour. Form dough into two 8 inch logs and roll in the coconut flakes. Wrap logs in parchment or wax paper and freeze. Slice and bake at 375 degrees for about twelve minutes. This makes about sixty cookies.

Author Note:

Excellent year round but best at Christmas. My neighbors stand at the door waiting for these to come out of the oven.

Susanne Marie Knight
http://www.susanneknight.com

Adulterous Apricot Á la Mode

Ingredients:

1 can apricots, drained, saving syrup
1 lemon
1/3 cup apricot marmalade or jelly
vanilla ice cream

Directions:

Pour 1/3 cup of syrup from apricots into pot.
Add the juice of 1 lemon and 1/3 cup marmalade or jelly.
Stir frequently and bring to boil.
Let cool.
Scoop ice cream into sherbet dishes and top with one or two canned apricots.
Pour syrup over dessert and serve.

Note: In my best-selling romantic suspense TAINTED TEA FOR TWO, the color of Greg's apricot marmalade reminds him of Kitty's vivid red hair. This simple recipe will remind you of just how delicious apricots can be!

Susanne Marie Knight
http://www.susanneknight.com

Lace Brownies

Ingredients:

1 cup white sugar
1/2 tsp. salt
1/2 cup brown sugar
1 tbsp. flour
1 cup quick cooking oatmeal
1 egg, beaten
1 square unsweetened chocolate
1/2 tsp. vanilla

Directions:

Preheat oven to 325 degrees.
Using low heat, melt chocolate square.
Mix ingredients in bowl to form batter.
Cover cookie sheet with aluminum foil.
Drop tsp. of batter on sheet and press down a bit.
Bake until golden brown, about ten minutes.
Remove, then cool.
Peel cookies from foil and store in a covered tin to keep crisp.

Note: In my futuristic science fiction romance ALIEN HEAT, impetuous Will Flagg loves the taste of lace brownies. You will too after you try these delicious cookies!

Susanne Marie Knight
http://www.susanneknight.com

Orapple or Ambrosia

Ingredients:

1 can (11 oz.) mandarin oranges, drained (save liquid)
Flaked coconut
1 apple, chopped
Confectioners' sugar
2 bananas, sliced

Directions:

Toss orange segments, apple pieces, and bananas.
Serve in sherbet cups.
Sprinkle with confectioners' sugar, coconut, and saved mandarin orange liquid.

Note: In the best-selling, award-winning science fiction romance JANUS IS A TWO-HEADED GOD, orapples (a genetic combination of orange and apple) only exist on the GCC home planet Xaspaar.
Here's a recipe that can be made and enjoyed on planet Earth that has the same out-of-this world taste!

Sylvie Kaye
www.sylviekaye.com

Whiskey Cake

Ingredients & Directions:

350 degrees for 1 hour

1 pkg. yellow cake mix
1 pkg. instant pudding
4 eggs
1 cup water
1/2 cup oil
1 cup nuts, chopped

Mix all ingredients. Pour into bundt pan. Bake at 350 degrees for an hour.

Melt: 1/2 cup sugar
1/2 cup whiskey
1/4 lb. oleo

Pour over hot cake. Let stand.

Larissa Lyons
www.larissalyons.com

Larissa's Luscious Layers
(original recipe from Larissa Lyons)

Ingredients:

1 stick butter
2 cup finely chopped pecans (or walnuts), separated
2 cup chocolate morsels (I use a mix of milk chocolate and semi-sweet; but white chocolate, bittersweet or even peanut butter will work, too! Heck, throw in another 1/2 cup if you want to!)
1 cup of shredded coconut (or, substitute more chocolate if you don't like coconut)
1 can of sweetened condensed milk (such as Eagle Brand)
3 tbsp. brown sugar, separated

Directions:

Heat oven to 330 degrees. In a glass 13"x9" dish, melt the butter (I do this in the oven while it's warming up).

Remove pan from oven and layer the remaining ingredients in the following order:
1 1/2 cups of the nuts (save 1/2 c for later)
Sprinkle on 2 T of the brown sugar
Add the chocolate morsels
Toss on the shredded coconut

Author Note:

Here's a yummy treat, full of gooey chocolate, nuts, and sugar...100% delicious.

Pour the sweetened condensed milk over everything, then top with the remaining 1/2 cup of chopped nuts and 1 T brown sugar.

Bake for 32 minutes or until the top is golden brown. Yum!!

Kate Fellowes
www.swimmingkangaroo.com/shadows.html

Desa's Cocoa Cake

Ingredients:

3 cups flour
1 1/2 cups sugar
1 tsp. salt
2 tsp. baking soda
6 tbsp. Nestle baking cocoa
2 tbsp. vinegar
1/2 cup oil
3 tsp. vanilla extract
2 cups water
1 cup coconut flakes

Directions:

Preheat oven to 350 degrees. Sift together flour, sugar, salt, baking soda and cocoa. Next add vinegar, oil, vanilla and water. Blend thoroughly so that not a single lump exists! Then, fold in coconut flakes. Oil and flour a 9" x 14" pan. Bake for 30 minutes, or until toothpick comes out clean.

Author Note:

My husband, novelist Jim Alexander and I used this recipe for our vegan wedding cake. It's a delicious chocolate cake made without eggs. It originally came from a friend of mine whose family is from Eastern Europe. I guess it's traditional there.

Susan Elizabeth Phillips
www.susanephillips.com

FIRST LADY Fruit Cocktail Cake

Preheat Oven to 350 degrees. Mix the following ingredients in an ungreased 8X8X2 inch cake pan.

1 cup flour
1 cup sugar
1/4 tsp. baking soda
1 egg
1/2 tsp. vanilla
1 can (8 1/4 oz.) fruit cocktail (undrained)
Optional: 1/2 cup chopped nuts

Bake 30 minutes. Frost immediately.

FROSTING: (My old notes say not to double for double recipe.)
1/4 cup butter, softened
1 pkg. (3 oz.) cream cheese softened
1 cup confectioners sugar sifted
1/2 tsp. vanilla
Blend all ingredients together until smooth. Frost cake while warm.

Author Note:

So much for healthy eating! Last month I received an e-mail from a reader asking for the recipe to the "Fruit Cocktail Cake" referred to in *FIRST LADY*. This is a dessert I made in the late 70s or early 80s and haven't made since. Please e-mail me if you try it and let me know how it is.

Susan Elizabeth Phillips
www.susanephillips.com

SUGAR BETH'S Chocolate Brownie Trifle
(Offered with apologies from SEP)

Ingredients:

1 brownie mix prepared in 13x9x2 pan and cut into 1" pieces

1 pkg. (4 serving size) chocolate fudge INSTANT pudding and pie filling mix PREPARED. (Or prepackaged chocolate pudding, if you're short on time)

1 small jar caramel ice cream topping (Sugar Beth uses Smuckers)

1 (8 oz.) container Cool Whip

(Nuts optional)

Directions:

Mix container of Cool Whip with about 3/4 of jar of caramel topping.

In a trifle dish or pretty glass bowl, layer half the brownies in the bottom. Add half the prepared pudding, then some of the caramel/whipped cream topping. Repeat. You'll end up with a little left over caramel/whipped cream topping. Wash down the sink. Do not eat like me! You can put nuts between layers. Instead, Sugar Beth toasts almonds or pecans and puts them in separate dish for people to use as optional topping. Cover and refrigerate at least 4 hours but not more than 24. This serves about 12-18 people depending on how piggy everybody is.

Author Note:

I had a big argument with Sugar Beth Carey, the heroine of *AIN'T SHE SWEET?*, about posting this recipe. I'm a nutrition nut and this recipe is nothing but JUNK!!!! Except, as Sugar Beth rightly pointed out, it's delicious junk. Thanks to Sugar Beth, this has become the Phillips Family Special Occasions Only Dessert. (And doesn't that woman know all kinds of ways to make trouble?!)

Rhonda Nelson
www.readrhondanelson.com

Mom's Banana Pudding

Ingredients:

1 cup sugar
1/2 cup all-purpose flour
1/2 tsp. salt
2 cups evaporated milk
1 tsp. vanilla
1 tbsp. butter
4 egg yolks
1 box vanilla wafers
4-5 bananas

Directions:

Mix first 3 ingredients in heavy pan. Gradually add milk. Cook on medium heat, stirring constantly until thick. (Add some hot pudding to beaten egg yolks, stir well and return to pan.) Cook one more minute, then add butter and vanilla. Layer cookies and pudding, add meringue and bake until golden on top.

Sydney Croft
www.SydneyCroft.com

Remy Begnaud's Cherry Bounce

2 qt. cherries, stemmed and cleaned
3 cups white sugar
1 qt. bourbon (but only because moonshine is hard to come by)

Place cherries in 1 gallon crock, glass bowl, or heavy bucket. Add sugar, stir. Cover crock with cloth. Stir ever other day. Let stand in sugar about 2 weeks. Then add 1 quart bourbon. Let set overnight, then strain through cotton cloth into bottles for use later, or into pitcher/tub/bowl for immediate use. Serve over ice.

Author Note: A favorite at Mardi Gras, wedding receptions, and pretty much any celebration...

Janice Maynard
www.janicemaynard.com

Sock-It To Me Cake

Mix all these ingredients... one package of Duncan Hines Butter Cake Mix (dry), 4 eggs, 3/4 cup of oil, 8 ounces of sour cream, 1/2 cup of sugar. No particular time... just blend with mixer or even a spoon until the ingredients are combined. In a separate bowl, mix two tablespoons of cinnamon with 4 tablespoons of brown sugar, set aside. Pour half of the batter in a Bundt pan. Sprinkle half of the brown sugar mixture over the batter. Add the rest of the batter, top with the remainder of the brown sugar mixture. Bake one hour at 300 degrees. Cool ten minutes before removing from pan. If you choose, you can add a cup of chopped nuts to the brown sugar mixture, but my family likes it without.

Rosemary Laurey
www.rosemarylaurey.com

Frangipan

Ingredients:

6-7 oz. roll or can of almond paste.
8 oz. unsalted butter at room temperature
3/4 cup sugar
3 eggs at room temperature
1/2 cup sifted cake flour
Pinch of salt (sifted with the flour)

Directions:

Butter and flour a 9" springform cake pan, using about 1" butter cut from one of the sticks.

Pre heat oven to 325 degrees.

Cream butter and almond paste together.
Add sugar, beat until smooth.
Add the eggs one at a time, beating well.
(A food processor or mixer works well for the above steps)

Add the sifted flour very, very gently. Just enough to mix it.
Bake 40 minute in the pre-heated oven. Cake will still be moist in the middle.

Let cool completely (best overnight) before removing from the cake pan.

Note: This is a very rich, dense and close-textured cake.

Rosemary Laurey
www.rosemarylaurey.com

Peach Pie

Ingredients:

1 baked pie shell
2 sticks unsalted butter.
I cup confectioner's sugar
Almond essence
Six ripe peaches
I cup Whipping cream
Sugar
Lemon juice.

Directions:

Cream the butter and the confectioner's sugar and spread over the bottom of the baked pie shell.

Peel and slice the peaches.
Dip slices in lemon juice to stop them from darkening.
Arrange slices on top of the cream filling.
Whip cream and sweeten to taste and spread on top of the peach layer.
Keep chilled.

LuAnn McLane
www.luannmclane.com

Dutch Apple Pannekoeken

Prep: 15 Minutes
Bake: 23 Minutes

Ingredients:

1/4 cup packed brown sugar
1/4 tsp. ground cinnamon
2 medium cooking apples, peeled and thinly sliced (about 2
   cups)
1/3 cup water
2 tbsp. butter
1/2 cup Original Bisquick
2 eggs

Directions:

Heat oven to 400 degrees. Generously grease pie plate, 9x1 1/4 inches. Mix brown sugar and cinnamon in medium bowl. Add apples, toss and set aside.

Heat water and butter to boiling in 2-quart saucepan; reduce heat to low. Add Bisquick; stir vigorously until mixture forms a ball. Remove from heat; beat in eggs, one at a time. Continue beating until smooth.

Spread batter in bottom of pie plate. Arrange apples on top to within 1 inch of edge of pie plate. Bake about 23 minutes or until puffed and edges are golden brown. Serve immediately. 6 servings.

Author Note:

This Dutch/German treat smells heavenly while baking. I usually dust with powdered sugar and add a dollop of whipped cream for good measure.

Lisa Freeman - Reader
"This pudding is just as tasty as the heroes in
a Janice Maynard novel."

Banana Pudding

Ingredients:

1 cup sugar
1/3 cup self-rising flour
3 eggs
2 cups milk
1/2 tsp. vanilla extract
Nilla Wafers
Bananas (ripe)

Directions:

Combine sugar and flour in large boiler. Beat eggs, mix well
with sugar/flour. Add milk. Cook over low heat until thickened,
stirring constantly. Remove from heat, add vanilla. Layer with
wafers and bananas.

Jennifer Pressley - Reader
"This desert will cool you down while you are reading a hot Lori Foster book."

Caramel Ice Cream Desert

Ingredients:

One box mini Ice cream sandwiches
1 Large Tub Cool Whip
1 package of 10 small Butterfinger candy bars
Caramel sauce in the squeeze bottle

Author Note:

I usually make this desert in a big deep round Rubbermaid container. The amount of ingredients is dependent on the size desert you want to make. I use 20 oz. of cool whip. If your container is big enough for 2 layers, get 2 large tubs of Cool Whip and 2 bottles of carmel sauce.

Directions:

Take the candy bars and put them into 2 Ziploc bags (5 bars will fit in a sandwich size bag).
Crunch them up with a hammer (it gets out the frustrations).
Layer the bottom of the container with ice cream sandwiches.
Put a layer of Coolwhip on top of the ice cream sandwiches.
Pour a layer of the caramel sauce on top of the cool whip.
Take the crunched up pieces of the candy bar in one Ziploc bag and spread on top of the caramel sauce.
If your container is deep enough, put another layer of cool whip, caramel sauce, and crunched up candy bars.
Put it into the freezer.

Larissa Ione
www.LarissaIone.com

Sneaky Pete

Ingredients:

750 ml 100 proof vodka
16 oz. pomegranate or cranberry juice
12 oz. frozen orange juice concentrate
12 oz. frozen lemonade
750 ml Fresca
1 cup powdered confectioner's sugar (optional)

Directions:

Mix all ingredients in large container with lid. Freeze approximately 2 days. Will be slushy.

Author Note:

Sneaky Petes are a holiday tradition in my husband's family, but they are great for parties, guests, and summertime as well. And they are called "sneaky" for a reason! ;)

Tori Carrington
www.toricarrington.net / www.sofiemetro.com

Galaktoboureko – Greek Custard Dessert

Ingredients:

6 cups whole milk
1 cup fine semolina (farina)
1 1/2 cups sugar
1 tbsp. flour
1 tbsp. vanilla
1 stick unsalted butter (1/2 cup)
6 egg yolks
25 phyllo sheets, thawed
3/4 cup melted butter (to brush phyllo sheets)

Syrup:
2 cups sugar
1 cup water
1 tsp. vanilla
1 tsp. fresh lemon juice
2 thin strips of lemon peel

Directions:

Combine semolina (farina), sugar and vanilla in a bowl. In a saucepan, bring the milk to a boil, stirring to prevent scorching. Slowly add semolina mix to the boiling milk. Cook over medium heat, stirring constantly, until the mixture thickens and comes to a full boil. Remove from the heat.

In a small bowl, beat the egg yolks with a fork, and then stir into the hot custard mixture.

Butter a 9" x 13" Pyrex baking pan and cover bottom with 10 sheets of the phyllo, brushing melted butter on each sheet as you go (sheets should extend up the sides of the pan). Pour the custard mixture on top. Cover with remaining phyllo sheets, brushing each with butter as you go.

Score the top phyllo sheets into square or diamond shapes, being careful not to score as deeply as the custard. Bake on the center rack of 375 degree oven for 35 to 40 minutes, until golden. Cut pieces all the way through.

Syrup: Boil two cups sugar with one-cup water, vanilla, lemon juice and lemon peel for 5 minutes. Ladle the hot syrup over the top.

Cool thoroughly before serving. Refrigerate in hot weather. Opa!

Rosemary Laurey
www.rosemarylaurey.com

Poached Pears

Ingredients & Directions:

For this recipe I use the brown skinned winter pears (Bosc or Conference)
Allow one pear per person.
Peel the pears and take a small slice off the bottoms so the pears stand upright without wobbling.
Arrange the pears in a lidded baking or roasting dish deep enough to hold them.
Pour over white wine (or apple juice) to a depth of about two inches, and add 1/2 tsp. of ground ginger per pear.
Cover with lid or aluminum foil and bake at 300 degrees for 45 minutes to 1 hour depending on size of pears.
Pears are done when a fork penetrates them easily.
Can be served warm, room temperature or chilled.

Larissa Ione
www.LarissaIone.com

Easy Cheesecake

Ingredients:

1 (8 oz. pkg.) cream cheese, softened
1/3 cup sugar
8 oz. Cool Whip
1 graham cracker crust

Directions:

Mix together cream cheese and sugar with electric mixer until smooth. Fold in Cool Whip with spatula. Spoon into crust and chill several hours. Can be served plain or with fruit topping, if desired.

Author Note:

This is super simple and perfect for those last-minute guests and potlucks. I always keep the ingredients on hand, just in case!

Amber Green
www.shapeshiftersinlust.com

Cheesecake with Pecan Crust

Crust:
1 cup all-purpose flour (graham flour works fine)
1/2 cup butter, softened
1/2 cup pecans, finely chopped, measured after you pick
    out the dark pieces and the spongy light-brown stuff
1/4 cup sugar.

Heat oven to 400 degrees.

Mix all ingredients. Mash to an even layer lining a 9" deep pie pan.

Bake 10-12 minutes. Turn oven down to 350, remove crust, and get to work on filling.

Filling:
1 lb. cream cheese
2 eggs
1 cup sugar
4 tsp. pure vanilla extract. (If you have imitation vanilla, blend 2 tsp. of it with 1 tsp. rum extract and 1 tsp. almond extract.)
2 cups sour cream

Directions:

Soften cream cheese and blend with eggs, half the sugar, and half the vanilla extract or vanilla blend. Spread in pecan crust and bake 20 minutes.

While it bakes, blend other ingredients. When the oven dings, remove cheesecake and turn the heat back up to 400 degrees. Spread sweetened sour cream over pie and give the oven time to get up to temp, then pop pie back in for JUST 5 minutes.

Serve cool or room temperature. It's supposed to be better the next day, but who on earth would know?

CITRUS/PECAN Variation: Mix grated kumquat zest, key lime zest, or grapefruit zest in with cream cheese.

PEACH/ALMOND Variation: Replace pecans with crushed toasted almonds and reduce crust's sugar by half. Add tiniest jar baby food pureed peaches to cream cheese part of mix, and replace vanilla with 1/2 vanilla and 1/2 almond extract.

Kathy Andrico – Reader
"Fantasy Fudge is Pure decadence—perfect when reading about a brooding, Dark Hunter or Carpathian hero."

Fantasy Fudge
A Previous Version from
Kraft Jet-Puffed Marshmallow Crème

Ingredients:

3 cups sugar
3/4 cup (1 & 1/2 sticks) butter (Parkay)
5 fl oz. (1 small can or about 2/3 cup) evaporated milk
12 oz. (2 cups) semi sweet chocolate chips
1 jar (7 oz) Kraft Jet-Puffed Marshmallow Cream
1 tsp. vanilla
Dash salt (optional)
1 cup chopped walnuts (optional)

Directions:

Butter a 9x13 pan. Set aside.
Combine sugar, butter, evaporated milk, and salt (optional). Bring to boil. Cook at boil for 4-5 minutes at medium heat, stirring constantly. Remove from heat. Add chocolate and stir until completely melted and thoroughly blended. Add marshmallow cream and vanilla. Stir until completely mixed. Add walnuts (optional).
Pour into buttered 9x13 pan. Set aside until firm—or enjoy immediately!

Author Note:

The current recipe on the back of the Kraft Jet-Puffed Marshmallow Cream Fantasy Fudge has been revised from this recipe.

Michelle M. Pillow
www.michellepillow.com

Michelle's Magik Bars

Ingredients:

2 cups graham cracker crumbs (or for faster preparation, two pre-made graham cracker pie crust)
1/2 cup butter, melted
1 cup semisweet chocolate chips
1 cup either white chocolate chips or butterscotch chips
1 cup flaked coconut
1 cup chopped pecans or walnuts (optional)
1 (14 oz.) can sweetened condensed milk

Directions:

Preheat oven to 325 degrees (165 degrees C).
Combine the graham cracker crumbs and melted butter. Press into the bottom of a 9x9 inch baking pan. Layer the chocolate chips, whiter chocolate or butterscotch chips, coconut and nuts over the crumbs. Pour the sweetened condensed milk over the top. (If using pie crusts, dot butter over the bottom and split ingredients in half per crust)
Bake at 325 degrees (165 degrees C) for 25 to 30 minutes. Let cool and cut into squares.

Author Note:

These are also called Hello Dollys or Seven Layer Bars and very easy to make in a hurry. If I, a mess in the kitchen, can make them—anyone can!

Kathy Andrico - Reader
When I eat one of Sharon's Lemon Cookies, I like to savor each bite. They are purely good, just like a romance by Cathy Liggett or Shelley Galloway.

Lemon Cookie
Provided by Sharon's Homemade Cookies and Treats
sharonlsiegfried@aol.com

Yield: approx. 2 dozen cookies
Ingredients:

1 pkg. (~18 oz) lemon cake mix (Duncan Hines recommended)
1/3 cup water
1/4 cup softened butter (room temperature)
1 egg, large
1 tbsp. freshly grated lemon zest (one average-sized lemon's worth)
1 cup (or more, if you wish) lemon chips or white chocolate chips
(Up to 1/4 cup flour can be added if dough is extremely sticky)
1/2 cup sugar for rolling

Directions:

Mix the cake mix, water, butter, egg, and lemon zest at low-speed until well blended. Warnings:
1.) Lemon zest will clump around beaters, so be sure to scrape well!
2.) Dough will be extremely sticky; it's okay to add up to 1/4 cup of flour to help.

Stir in the chips. Chill the dough overnight to reduce stickiness and allow the flavor to develop.
Roll tbsp.-sized balls of dough in sugar (you may have to wet your hands to work with the dough), place on parchment-paper lined cookie sheets, and bake for 12-14 minutes at 350 degrees.

Paige Cuccaro
www.paigecuccaro.com / www.alisonpaige.net

Strawberry Pretzel Dessert

Ingredients:

2 cups pretzel sticks, broken up
3 tbsp. sugar
3/4 cup melted butter
1 (8 oz.) cream cheese
1 cup sugar
1 large Cool Whip
1 large strawberry Jello
2 cups boiling water
2 (10oz.) pkg. frozen strawberries

Directions:

Mix first 3 ingredients and place in 9 x 13-inch pan. Bake at 400 degrees for 8 minutes. Set aside and cool.

Beat Sugar into cream cheese and stir in Cool Whip. Spread on cool pretzels and refrigerate.

Mix together last 3 ingredients and let stand until it begins to gel. Gently pour over cheese mixture and refrigerate.

Patti Foster - Reader
"These sweets are almost as good as digging into your favorite novel!"

Peanut Butter Fingers

Cream:
1/2 cup butter (or margarine)
1/2 cup sugar
1/2 cup brown sugar (firmly packed)

Blend in:
1 egg
1/3 cup peanut butter
1/2 tsp. soda
1/4 tsp. salt
1/2 tsp. vanilla

Stir In:
1 cup flour
1 cup QuickCook Rolled Oats

Spread in greased 13 x 9 pan. Bake at 350 degrees for 20-25 min.

Sprinkle with 1 cup Nestles Semi-Sweet choc chips (6 oz. pkg). Let stand 5 min to melt (I turn off oven and leave door open, sit pan in there! Is quicker!)

Spread chocolate and let cool

Ice with Peanut Butter icing. (make one cut lengthwise down the center of the pan, then cut about 1 1/4" slices across this...makes the "fingers"! More distinctive cut than brownies!!!)

Peanut Butter icing:
1/2 cup powdered sugar
1/4 cup Peanut Butter
2-4 tbsp. milk

You can also use this combination to make icing for chocolate cake. Just keep mixing the ingredients until you have enough! Add more milk to thin, or more sugar to thicken! If you like peanut butter and chocolate, you'll love this! It's been a favorite of my entire family since I was a child!

Danielle Devon
www.danielledevon.com

Espresso Toffee Fudge

Ingredients:

Butter-flavored cooking spray
1 stick butter
4 cups sugar
1 (12 oz.) can evaporated milk
2 tbsp. instant espresso powder
1 (12-oz.) package semisweet chocolate chips
30 large marshmallows
3/4 cup toffee bits

Directions:

Lightly coat 9 by 13-inch baking pan with butter-flavored cooking spray. In a large saucepan over medium heat, combine butter, sugar, evaporated milk, and espresso powder. Stirring constantly, bring to a rolling boil for 10 minutes. Remove from heat and stir in chocolate chips and marshmallows until blended. Pour into prepared pan. Sprinkle toffee chips evenly over fudge and pat lightly. Cool until set, about 3 to 4 hours. Cut into bite-sized squares.

Jennah Sharpe
www.jennahsharpe.com

No-Bake Toblerone Cheesecake

Ingredients:

1 1/4 cups Oreo Baking Crumbs
1/4 cup melted butter
2 pkg. (250 g. each) cream cheese, softened
1 cup smooth peanut butter
1 cup sugar
2 bars (100 g. each) Toblerone Swiss milk chocolate, divided
1 1/2 cups thawed cool whip topping

Directions:

Mix crumbs and butter; press firmly onto bottom o f 9-inch springform pan. Refrigerate 10 minutes.

Beat cream cheese, peanut butter and sugar with electric mixer on medium speed until well blended. Chop 1 bar of the chocolate; stir into cream cheese mixture. Gently stir in 1 cup of the whipped topping. Spoon over crust. Refrigerate 3 hours.

Microwave remaining 1/2 cup whipped topping and 1 bar chocolate in small microwaveable bowl on HIGH 1 minute. Stir until chocolate is melted and mixture well blended; cool slightly. Pour over cake. Refrigerate until ready to serve.

Makes 12 servings, 1 slice each

This is a super easy chocolaty cheesecake that doesn't need to be baked. It received rave reviews at Christmas.

J.C. Wilder / Dominique Adair
www.jcwilder.com / www.dominiqueadair.com

Brownie Decadence

Ingredients:

Butter for ramekins
3/4 cup semisweet chocolate chips
4 oz. unsalted butter
2 large eggs
3/4 cup powdered sugar
3 tbsp. flour
1/2 cup white chocolate chips
1 tsp. vanilla

Directions:

Preheat oven to 400 degrees. Butter four 2/3 cup ramekins and set aside.

Using a double boiler, melt the butter and semisweet chocolate chips and set aside to cool.

In a separate bowl, mix together eggs, sugar, flour and vanilla. Add cooled chocolate mixture and mix until blended. Fold in white chocolate chips.

Divide between the ramekins, place on baking sheet. Bake 20 minutes until tops are shiny and cracked (the insides will be hot and gooey).

Author Note:

When I say decadent, I mean...decadent. I only use this recipe for special occasions. The center of these desserts will be hot and gooey and they should be served warm. Perfect with a glass of ice cold milk. You can used flavored chocolate chips—I've never tried it but I don't see why it wouldn't work.

Jo Dartlon
www.DartlonDesigns.com
Affordable graphic and website designs

MeMe's Strawberry Dream Pie-DELICIOUS!

1/2 cup sugar
1 cup water
3 tbsp. cornstarch
4 tbsp. strawberry Jello
1 qt. sliced strawberries
1 container of whipped topping
1 pie crust (graham cracker or regular-If you're in a rush, the store-bought brands work great in this recipe.)

Mix sugar, water and cornstarch. Bring to a boil, stirring constantly. Remove from heat. (You can add a drop or two of red food coloring here for a beautiful deep red filling) Add Jello and strawberries and cool to lukewarm. Fold in whipped topping. Pour in pie shell and chill.

Graham cracker crust:
1-2/3 cups graham crackers, ground
1/4 cup sugar
1/4 cup plus 2 T. butter or margarine

Melt butter or margarine. Combine all ingredients, mixing well. Firmly press crumb mixture evenly over bottom and sides of a 9 inch pie plate. Bake at 350 degrees F. for 7 to 9 minutes. Makes one 9 inch crust

Pie Crust:
1 cups all purpose flour
1/2 cup Crisco shortening (preferably cold)
Pinch of salt
2 tbsp. ice water

Mix dry ingredients Cut in shortening with pastry cutter or fork. Add ice water and continue working until dough forms, but don't overwork.
Makes 1 9-inch pie crust.

Author Note:

My Mom used to make this pie for us on those scorching hot summer days when I was growing up in Oklahoma. That first bit felt like pure heaven! It's light and refreshing with a creamy filling that simply melts in your mouth.

Al Foster
(Lori Foster's husband)

Oreo Cookie Cake

Ingredients:

1 1/4 lb. Oreo cookies
1 stick margarine
2 large boxes of vanilla instant pudding mix
3 1/2 cup cold milk
3 oz. cream cheese
1 small container of Cool Whip

Directions:

Crumble cookies and put some in the bottom of pan (enough to cover bottom).

Melt one stick of margarine and pour over crumbled cookies.

Mix boxes of pudding mix, cold milk, and softened cream cheese. Beat until thick. Spread over crumbled cookies.

Spread one small container of Cool Whip on top, then sprinkle on the rest of the crumbled cookies.

Let set 30 minutes before eating.

Lisa Freeman - Reader
A dessert that's as tasty as your favorite
LuAnn McLane book!

Banana Pudding

1 cup sugar
1/3 cup self-rising flour
3 eggs
2 cups milk
1/2 tsp. vanilla extract
Nilla Wafers
Bananas (ripe)

Combine sugar and flour in large boiler. Beat eggs, mix well with sugar/flour. Add milk. Cook over low heat until thickened, stirring constantly. Remove from heat, add vanilla. Layer with wafers and bananas.

Laurie Damron - Reader
This fudge sauce is absolutely decadent, just
like your favorite Lori Foster novel!

Hot Fudge Sauce

1 cup sugar
1 heaping tbsp. cocoa
1 can evaporated milk
3 tbsp. butter

Mix all ingredients and cook at medium heat until it comes to a boil, stirring constantly. After it begins to boil turn off heat and add 1 tsp. vanilla. Serve warm.

Cryna Palmiere - Reader
A favorite dessert to go with one of my favorite romance books.

Apple Pudding

Ingredients & Directions:

1 cup flour
1 tsp. baking powder
1/2 cup milk
1/2 cup white sugar
1/2 tsp. vanilla
4-6 peeled apples (depending on size)

Mix flour, baking powder, milk, white sugar and vanilla in bottom of oven proof bowl. Slice peeled apples into this mixture and stir enough to coat apples nicely.

Then add to top of mixture, but not stirring:

1/2 cup brown sugar
2 cups boiling water
Piece of butter or margarine (size of an egg)

Bake at 350 degree, preheated oven until apples and cake batter are nicely browned.

Serve hot as a dessert. Tastes good with ice cream scooped on top.

Cryna Palmiere - Reader
A tasty dessert to go with a tasty Jayne Ann Krentz novel.

Feather Cup Cakes

Ingredients:

2 eggs
1 cup sour milk
1 cup white sugar
1/2 cup butter/margarine
1 tsp. vanilla
2 cups flour
2 tsp. baking powder

Directions:

Cream butter and sugar. Add beaten eggs. Then milk (you can make milk sour by adding a little vinegar).

Sift flour and baking powder together and stir into the batter.

Pour into cup cake tins lined with cup cake wrappers. Bake in moderate oven (375 degrees) until done.

Frost as desired.

Laurie Damron - Reader
These cookies are reminiscent of a
Dianne Castell book; they're colorful and sweet!

M & M Cookies

Ingredients:

3/4 cup butter
1 1/3 cups firmly packed light brown sugar
2 eggs
1 tsp. vanilla
2 1/4 cups flour
1 tsp. soda
1/2 tsp. salt
1 cup M & Ms
1/2 cup chopped nuts

Directions:

Beat sugar and butter until light and fluffy, blend in eggs and vanilla. Gradually add flour, soda and salt. Mix well. Stir in candies and nuts. Drop by heaping tablespoons onto greased cookie sheet – 3" apart. Press 3-4 M&Ms® into each cookie if desired. Bake at 350 degrees for 10-12 min. Cool on cookie sheet for 3 min.

Gia Dawn
www.giadawn.com

This is in memory of
First Lieutenant Robert C. Perez US Air Force

Easy Chocolate Truffles

Ingredients:

1/2 cup heavy cream
8 oz. bittersweet chocolate cut into small chunks
6 tbsp. unsalted butter
Assorted sugars, nuts, etc... for rolling truffles in

Directions:

In small heavy saucepan bring cream to a boil. Remove from heat and stir in chocolate and butter, returning to heat for 30 seconds if necessary. Stir until chocolate and butter are completely melted.

Pour mixture into shallow glass or plastic dish and refrigerate until firm (approx. 2 hours). With a melon baller or fingers, roll the cold truffle mixture into balls, and then roll in powdered cocoa, powdered sugar, finely chopped nuts, or anything else that sounds yummy.

Place in airtight container lined with wax paper, with more wax paper to separate layers.

Author Note:

Bob loved to make these on Easter. He served in both WWII and the Korean War, and earned the Air Medal for his courage during combat. He passed away December 25, 2006, aged 88.

Rikki Morris – Reader
This dessert is every bit as tempting as a
Jayne Ann Krentz romance novel!

Cherries in the Clouds

Ingredients:
1 pkg. of softened cream cheese
1/2 cup sugar
2 cups thawed whipped topping
1 can (20 oz.) cherry pie filling

Prep:
Mix cream cheese and sugar until smooth. Gently stir in whipped topping. Layer 2 Tbsp. cream cheese mixture and 2 tbsp. pie filing in 8 oz. stemmed glasses or dessert cups. Repeat layers. Place one cherry on top to finish Cherries in the Clouds.
Serves 8, about 2/3 cup each

Jodi Shadden - Reader
"A sweet dessert to go with a spicy Janice Maynard novel!"

Cranberry Dessert

1 pkg. cranberries
1 bowl (9 oz.) cool whip
1/2 pkg. miniature marshmallows
1/2 cup chopped walnuts

Chop cranberries in blender. Pour cranberries into large bowl. Add sugar to the top and let sit 1 1/2 hours (minimum). Add cool whip, marshmallows, and walnuts.
Author Note: I usually prepare the cranberry and sugar mixture the night before I need this. It tends to make the dessert sweeter.

Billie Warren Chai

Ma Carlisle's Strawberry Cake

Ingredients & Directions:

1 Box White Cake Mix
1 Box Strawberry Jello
3/4 cup Wesson Oil
1/2 cup or less cold water
3/4 of 10 oz. box Frozen Strawberries
4 eggs
Mix all ingredients and pour into cake pan(s). Bake at 350 degrees for 30-35 minutes. Cool 10 minutes

ICING
1 Box Powdered Sugar
1 Stick softened butter
1/4 of 10 oz. box of Frozen Strawberries

Lucinda Betts
www.lucindabetts.com

Chocolate Chip Cookie Recipe

There are a lot of ways to a man's heart, but one way that's tried and true is through his stomach. Just ask your grandmother! And there's nothing that says old-fashioned competence like a plate of home-baked chocolate chip cookies. (These also work well after you've married him, had children, and need to tame the principal after your bundle of joy let his ant farm loose in the Kindergarten classroom!)

Ingredients:
2 sticks of butter
3/4 cups sugar

2 1/4 cups flour
3/4 cups brown sugar
1 egg
1 tsp. baking soda
1 tsp. salt
2 tbsp. cherry snow-cone flavoring (blueberry flavoring, maraschino cherry juice, or vanilla works well, too)
2 cups chocolate chips

Directions:
350 degrees. Put butter and sugar in mixer and let mix until the mixture is fluffy. Add the flour, brown sugar, egg, baking soda, salt and flavor. Mix well. Add the chocolate chips and mix just a little bit. You don't want to crush them. Put a small ball of dough on tray and cook for 8 minutes.

Tricks:

Using a snow cone flavor gives your cookies an exotic flavor that people love but can't place. Try it once, and you'll never go back.

Get your cookie pans from Williams Sonoma or some other high-end place. The cookies bake more evenly and everyone will think your cookies seem like they came from a bakery. Remember when you use these trays that the cookies keep baking when you take them out of the oven. When you take them out after 8 minutes, you might think they're not cooked enough. Let them sit on the tray until they're cool, and they'll be perfect.

You can make your cookies look professional by shaping the dough into a snake shape and pulling a bit off the end before putting it on the tray to bake. If you make a skinny snake, you get lots of small cookies. If you make a fat snake, you get fewer big cookies. If you use this method, all of the cookies will be the same perfect size. While the man of your dreams won't care, the Kindergarten teacher will definitely notice your attention to detail!

Jean Marie Ward
www.wardsmith.com

Annette's Slovak Apple Pie

Ingredients:

(Note: Recipe amounts based on a rectangular pan, roughly 12x8x2 inches.)

Crust:

3 cups flour
1 tsp. baking powder
1/4 tsp. cinnamon
1/2 tsp. salt
2 tbsp. sugar
1/2 lb. butter
1/4-1/2 cup cold milk (or more, as needed)
Additional flour for rolling dough

Filling:

6 cups apples, peeled, cored and sliced (or enough to fill the pan with a little mound in the center)
1/2 cup unseasoned cracker or bread crumbs
1-1 1/4 cup sugar (depending on the sweetness of the apples)
2 tbsp. butter
Cinnamon
1-2 tbsp. flour (only if the apples are very juicy)

Directions:

Start the crust by sifting the measured flour, baking powder, cinnamon, salt and sugar together. Add the butter. Mix together with a pastry cutter or two knives (one held in each hand) until the mixture is reduced to even bits of dough about the size of peas. Sprinkle the milk over the dough until you can pat the dough into a large ball. (This part can be done with your hands if you work fast.) Wrap the dough in wax paper or plastic wrap and chill for at least a half hour before rolling the crust on a generously floured surface. Use about 5/8 of the dough for the bottom crust, and don't be afraid of pushing and patching it in the corners. Return the rolled top crust to the refrigerator while you prepare the filling.

Begin filling the pie by sprinkling the breadcrumbs on the bottom of the crust. Starting with a layer of apples, fill the crust with alternate layers of apples, sugar and cinnamon. Add a light dusting of flour if the apples are very juicy. Dot the final layer of sugar and cinnamon with butter. Cover with the top crust and seal the edges. Vent the crust by slashing or pricking it in a decorative pattern. Bake at 350 degrees until the apples are tender and the crust is brown, usually between 45 minutes and an hour. Let cool as long as you can stand it before cutting. Enjoy!

Author Note:

I don't know whether to blame *The Sopranos* or all those movies where people die face down in the clam linguini, but most Americans labor under the misconception all Italians can cook. Trust me, there is no Italian cooking gene. Take my mom. Better yet, take her cooking...*Please!*

When Hormel first marketed chili-injected hot dogs, strangers accosted Mom on the street, demanding to know what she did with her old hypodermics. Our family feasts generally required their own hazmat containment fields. My personal favorites were the Christmas turkey Mom imploded in an autoclave and her infamous Nagasaki Ribs. (*Blackened fingers of bone reaching toward the sky...* Well, that's what you get when you nuke pre-cooked spare ribs for an hour on high.)

My Slovak mother-in-law Annette, on the other hand, could make bread from scratch and cook a roast so tender you could cut it with the proverbial fork. This is her apple pie recipe. I expanded it to include the "lilli-bits" she *didn't* tell me. The recipe's unusual, because it ditches the customary thickeners in favor of bread crumbs, which let the natural flavors of the apples shine through. The rectangular pan became a family tradition because the standard-sized, round version of the pie never lasted long enough for leftovers.

Jean Marie Ward

Jean Marie's resume includes writing art books and celebrity interviews, editing a multi-genre web 'zine and government journals, and a stint as an associate producer on local access cable. No cooking shows, though. Her first novel, *With Nine You Get Vanyr*, written with the late Teri Smith, is published by Samhain Publishing, Ltd.

AUTHORS

AUTHORS

AUTHORS

READERS & OTHERS

Notes:

Notes:

Notes:

Notes:

Notes:

GREAT
CHEAP
FUN

Discover eBooks!
THE FASTEST WAY TO GET THE HOTTEST NAMES

Get your favorite authors on your favorite reader, long before they're out in print! Ebooks from Samhain go wherever you go, and work with whatever you carry—Palm, PDF, Mobi, and more.

Samhain
Publishing, ltd

WWW.SAMHAINPUBLISHING.COM